Protecting Competition
from the
Postal Monopoly

Protecting Competition
from the
Postal Monopoly

J. Gregory Sidak
Daniel F. Spulber

THE AEI PRESS

Publisher for the American Enterprise Institute
WASHINGTON, D.C.

1996

Available in the United States from the AEI Press, c/o Publisher Resources Inc., 1224 Heil Quaker Blvd., P.O. Box 7001, La Vergne, TN 37086-7001 or by phone at (800) 269-6267. Distributed outside the United States by arrangement with Eurospan, 3 Henrietta Street, London WC2E 8LU England.

To order copies of this volume on an overnight basis, call Amanda Riepe at AEI at (202) 862-5907.

Library of Congress Cataloging-in-Publication Data

Sidak, J. Gregory.
    Protecting competition from the postal monopoly / J. Gregory Sidak, Daniel F. Spulber.
            p.   cm.
    Includes bibliographical references and indexes.
    ISBN 0-8447-3950-2 (cloth : alk. paper)
      1. Privatization--United States. 2. United States Postal Service--Management. 3. Postal service--United States--Management.
4. Government Business enterprises--United States--Management.
5. Government monopolies--United States. I. Spulber, Daniel F.
II. Title.
HE6371.S55   1996
353.0087'3--dc20   95-40078
                                                                                       CIP

©1996 by the American Enterprise Institute for Public Policy Research, Washington, D.C. All rights reserved. No part of this publication may be used or reproduced in any manner whatsoever without permission in writing from the American Enterprise Institute except in the case of brief quotations embodied in news articles, critical articles, or reviews. The views expressed in the publications of the American Enterprise Institute are those of the authors and do not necessarily reflect the views of the staff, advisory panels, officers, or trustees of AEI.

THE AEI PRESS
Publisher for the American Enterprise Institute
1150 17th Street, N.W., Washington, D.C. 20036

Printed in the United States of America

To our children,

Gunnar and Christian

Rachelle, Aaron, and Benjamin

Contents

Acknowledgments *xi*

About the Authors *xiii*

1 The Dilemma of Postal Competition *1*

2 The Nature and Extent of the Postal Monopoly *11*
 The Private Express Statutes *13*
 *Third Class Mail and the
  Private Express Statutes* *18*
 *Exemptions from and Exceptions to the
  Private Express Statutes* *19*
 *Enforcement of the Private Express
  Statutes by the Postal Service* *31*
 The Regulation of Mailboxes *33*
 Conclusion *38*

3 Technological Justifications for the Postal Monopoly   *39*
    The Natural Monopoly Justification for the
        Public Postal Monopoly   40
    The Definition of Natural Monopoly   40
    Is the Postal Service a Natural Monopoly?   43
    The Fallacy That the Postal Service Must Be a
        Nationwide Full-Service Carrier   55
    Conclusion   60

4 Public Provision of Postal Services   *61*
    The Absence of Insurmountable Technological
        Barriers to Entry in Postal Delivery   63
    Cost Economies Do Not Justify Public
        Provision of Postal Services   66
    Public Provision Is Not Needed to Ensure
        Ubiquity and Pricing Uniformity   70
    Public Provision Is Not Needed to Ensure
        the Integrity of the Mail Stream   74
    Conclusion   81

5 Overseeing the Postal Monopoly   *83*
    Regulatory Control   84
    Managerial Control   88
    Congressional Oversight   95
    Executive Branch Oversight   96
    Conclusion   97

6 The Competitive Problems of Postal Service Pricing and Regulations   *101*
    Preventing Anticompetitive Cost Misallocation
        by the Postal Service   101

*Incorrect Measurement and Misallocation
    of Attributable Costs*   *105*
Misuse of Ramsey Pricing Principles   *124*
The Postal Service's Pursuit of "Profit"   *137*
Conclusion   *140*
*Appendix: Ramsey Pricing and
    Cost Misallocation*   *140*

7 Policy Recommendations   *147*
Acquiescence   *147*
Privatization   *151*
Commercialization   *152*
Stricter Public Oversight   *159*
Conclusion   *162*

References   *165*

Case and Regulatory Proceeding Index   *179*

Name Index   *183*

Subject Index   *187*

Acknowledgments

THIS BOOK GREW out of a report on the use of inverse elasticity pricing by the Postal Service that we prepared, at the request of United Parcel Service, for submission in June 1995 to the Subcommittee on the Postal Service of the House Committee on Government Reform and Oversight. The core of that analysis forms chapter 6 of this book. The views expressed there and throughout the book are exclusively our own.

We have benefited from the useful suggestions of participants in roundtable discussions of a draft of this book at the Federal Trade Commission and the American Enterprise Institute in September 1995. We also thank Jonathan B. Baker, Robert W. Crandall, Christopher DeMuth, Bert Ely, George R. Hall, John Hilke, Pauline Ippolito, Robert L. Kendall, Jr., Paul W. MacAvoy, William Ty Mayton, John E. McKeever, George L. Priest, Gary Roberts, James A. Rogers, Linda Shepherd, Michael G. Vita, and Mark Williams for their careful reading of the manuscript and their valuable comments. Finally, we wish to express our gratitude to Marshall Smith, Amanda Riepe, and Ian Connor, who provided useful research assistance and prepared the manuscript for publication.

J. GREGORY SIDAK
DANIEL F. SPULBER

About the Authors

J. GREGORY SIDAK is the F. K. Weyerhaeuser Fellow in Law and Economics at the American Enterprise Institute for Public Policy Research and Senior Lecturer at the Yale School of Management. He directs AEI's Studies in Telecommunications Deregulation and its Studies in Postal Regulation.

Mr. Sidak served as deputy general counsel of the Federal Communications Commission from 1987 to 1989, and as senior counsel and economist to the Council of Economic Advisers in the Executive Office of the President from 1986 to 1987. As an attorney in private practice, he worked on numerous antitrust cases and federal administrative, legislative, and appellate matters concerning regulated industries.

Mr. Sidak is coauthor, with William J. Baumol, of *Toward Competition in Local Telephony* (MIT Press & AEI Press 1994) and *Transmission Pricing and Stranded Costs in the Electric Power Industry* (AEI Press 1995). He is the editor of *Governing the Postal Service* (AEI Press 1994). He has published articles on antitrust, telecommunications regulation, corporate governance, and constitutional law in the *Journal of*

Political Economy, the *California Law Review*, the *Columbia Law Review*, the *Cornell Law Review*, the *Duke Law Journal*, the *Georgetown Law Journal*, the *Harvard Journal on Law & Public Policy*, the *New York University Law Review*, the *Northwestern University Law Review*, the *Southern California Law Review*, the *Yale Journal on Regulation*, and elsewhere.

Mr. Sidak received A.B. and A.M. degrees in economics and a J.D. from Stanford University, where he was a member of the *Stanford Law Review*, and served as law clerk to Judge Richard A. Posner during his first term on the U.S. Court of Appeals for the Seventh Circuit.

DANIEL F. SPULBER is the Thomas G. Ayers Professor of Energy Resource Management and professor of management strategy at the J. L. Kellogg Graduate School of Management, Northwestern University, where he has taught since 1990. He was previously professor of economics and professor of economics and law at the University of Southern California. He has also taught economics at Brown University and the California Institute of Technology.

Professor Spulber has conducted extensive research in the areas of regulation, industrial organization, microeconomic theory, energy economics, and management strategy. His scholarly research and consulting have addressed issues of regulation and competition in network industries. He is the author of the textbook *Regulation and Markets* (MIT Press 1989) and has published more than fifty articles on regulation, pricing, and related topics in numerous academic journals, including the *American Economic Review*, the *Journal of Economic Theory*, the *Journal of Law and Economics*, the *Quarterly Journal of Economics*, the *RAND Journal of Economics*, and the *Yale Journal on Regulation*. He is the founding editor of the *Journal of Economics & Management Strategy*, published by the MIT Press.

Professor Spulber received his B.A. in economics from the University of Michigan, and his M.A. and Ph.D. in economics from Northwestern University.

Protecting Competition
from the
Postal Monopoly

1

The Dilemma of Postal Competition

THE PRIVATE EXPRESS STATUTES protect the U.S. Postal Service from competition in the delivery of letter mail. In contrast, few if any corresponding rules protect competition in other areas from the federal government's postal monopoly. Not only are the Postal Service's competitive activities arguably unrestricted by any explicit application of antitrust law, but public ownership and control exempt the Postal Service's actions from the corporate governance that is characteristic of private enterprises. The Postal Service can take advantage of its autonomy and protected letter mail monopoly to subsidize its entry and expansion in competitive markets, such as parcel post and express mail. This raises a fundamental issue: whether Congress's grant of a monopoly to the Postal Service over the delivery of letter mail should be used to restrict or supplant private commerce in other markets. In this book, we examine the justifications for the publicly protected postal monopoly and its public ownership and control. On the basis of our economic and legal analysis, we demonstrate the need to prevent extension of the postal monopoly into competitive markets.

The Postal Service's privileges and immunities make it unique among economic enterprises. It pays no income taxes,[1] pays no dividends or return of invested capital to its owners,[2] and is not subject to the full enforcement powers of the Occupational Safety and Health Administration (OSHA).[3] In addition, the Postal Service may be entitled to have its leases and commercial contracts interpreted under federal common law rather than state law,[4] has the priority of the U.S. government with respect to the payment of debts from bankrupt estates,[5] and may borrow directly from the U.S. Treasury or may issue debt to third parties backed by the full faith and credit of the U.S. government.[6] Pursuant to the Private Express Statutes,

---

1. The statutory definition of "total estimated costs" of the Postal Service, which is used for ratemaking purposes, makes no mention of taxes. 39 U.S.C. § 3621.

2. *See id.*

3. OSHA may visit Postal Service sites and issue reports, but it cannot fine the Postal Service. *See* Peter G. Chronis, *Crucial Postal Machinery Cited by OSHA for Injuries*, DENVER POST, May 20, 1995, at B3; Kerri S. Smith, *Post Office to Start Injury-Prevention Plan*, ROCKY MOUNTAIN NEWS, Aug. 3, 1994, at 48A. Legislation that would have subjected the Postal Service to OSHA fines passed committee in 1994 but was not enacted. H.R. 115, 103d Cong., 2d Sess. (1994).

4. *See* Powers v. United States Postal Serv., 671 F.2d 1041 (7th Cir. 1982) (Posner, J.).

5. 39 U.S.C. § 401(9).

6. *Id.* §§ 2006(a), (c). According to Paul MacAvoy and George McIsaac:

> Capital has been available [for the Postal Service] from the Federal Financing Bank (FFB) . . . at interest charges less than market rates . . . . [T]he Postal Service . . . financed [its] placements of debt with the FFB in the 1970's, at a 12.5 basis-point premium above Treasury bond rates.

Paul W. MacAvoy & George S. McIsaac, *The Current File on the Case for Privatization of the Federal Government Enterprises*, 4 HUME PAPERS ON PUB. POL'Y (forthcoming 1995).

the Postal Service has a monopoly over the delivery of letters,[7] and it may engage in searches and seizures when it suspects that a competitor is transporting mail, or that a customer is sending mail in contravention of that monopoly.[8] Some advantages accorded the Postal Service are utterly arbitrary. For example, a taxpayer is not entitled to the legal presumption that he filed his tax return in a timely manner with the Internal Revenue Service if he uses a private carrier service such as Federal Express rather than the Postal Service.[9] Other privileges are simply bizarre: The Postal Service has been held to have the *constitutional* right to have its letter carriers take shortcuts across front lawns without obtaining the consent of the affected residents.[10]

The effectiveness of the legal and regulatory barriers to entry into mail delivery is evident. By any measure, the Postal Service is immense. As of 1994, it had annual sales of $49.4 billion, 728,944 career employees and an additional 123,101 noncareer employees, nearly 40,000 post offices, and 207,000 vehicles.[11] If ranked among the *Fortune* 500, the Postal Service would appear ahead of such corporations as Du Pont, Texaco, and Citicorp.[12] The Postal Service is larger than the three largest airlines—American, United, and Delta—*combined*.[13] It is larger than all five of the *Fortune* 1,000 package

---

7. 18 U.S.C. §§ 1693-99; 39 U.S.C. §§ 601-06.
8. 39 U.S.C. §§ 603-05; *see also id.* § 404(a)(7).
9. Petrulis *v.* Commissioner, 938 F.2d 78 (7th Cir. 1991) (construing 26 U.S.C. § 7502); Pugsley *v.* Commissioner, 749 F.2d 691 (11th Cir. 1985); *In re* Smith, 179 Bankr. 66 (W.D. Ohio 1995).
10. United States *v.* Pittsburg, 661 F.2d 783 (9th Cir. 1981).
11. U.S. POSTAL SERVICE, COMPREHENSIVE STATEMENT ON POSTAL OPERATIONS, FY 1994, at 10, 14, 17, 38 (1995); U.S. POSTAL SERVICE, 1994 ANNUAL REP. 3, 37 (1995).
12. *The Fortune 500 Largest U.S. Corporations*, FORTUNE, May 15, 1995, at 165.
13. *Id.* at F44.

4 Protecting Competition from the Postal Monopoly

and freight companies combined.[14] Indeed, as the Postal Service itself notes in its 1994 annual report, "Each of the Postal Service's seven product lines would qualify as a *Fortune* 500 company on its own."[15]

This large and privileged public enterprise also happens to compete in several product markets against private firms such as Airborne Express, DHL, Federal Express, and United Parcel Service. Some in government advocate that the Postal Service be awarded greater privileges to carry out further expansion. In 1992, the General Accounting Office (GAO) issued a report to Congress recommending legislation to grant the Postal Service greater pricing flexibility, through use of what economists call the inverse elasticity rule, "to maintain the long-term viability of the Postal Service as a nationwide full-service provider of postal services."[16] At the heart of the GAO's analysis were issues of cost allocation across classes of mail—issues so obscure and technical in appearance that they would put to sleep all but the most dedicated industrial organization economists and aficionados of postal rate regulation. The implication of the GAO report, however, was anything but dull, for the GAO was in effect

---

14. *Id*. at F58. In declining order of size, they are United Parcel Service, Federal Express, Pittston, Airborne Freight, and Air Express International.

15. U.S. POSTAL SERVICE, 1994 ANNUAL REP. 9 (1995). The product lines and their sizes, in terms of annual sales, are as follows: correspondence and transactions ($24.5 billion), business advertising ($12.7 billion), expedited delivery ($2.9 billion), standard package delivery ($2 billion), international mail ($1.4 billion), publications delivery ($1.7 billion), and retail ($3 billion). *Id.*

16. GENERAL ACCOUNTING OFFICE, U.S. POSTAL PRICING: PRICING POSTAL SERVICES IN A COMPETITIVE ENVIRONMENT 8 (1992). The GAO report followed by five months a consulting report commissioned by the Postal Service that warned of the adverse consequences for the Postal Service of losing market share in parcel post and overnight mail. INSTITUTE FOR PUBLIC ADMINISTRATION, THE RATEMAKING PROCESS FOR THE UNITED STATES POSTAL SERVICE 28-33 (report to the Board of Governors of the United States Postal Service, Oct. 1991).

recommending that the Postal Service be granted the freedom to be a more aggressive competitor of private firms in those classes of mail that are not currently guaranteed monopolies of the Postal Service under the Private Express Statutes.

The GAO's 1992 report found renewed relevance in January 1995, when Postmaster General Marvin Runyon stated in a speech to the National Press Club that the only kind of postal privatization he favored was that which, rather than selling off the Postal Service to private investors, would grant the public enterprise greater flexibility to cut prices to customers of competitive mail services—which include parcel post and overnight mail—and to introduce new products:

> With changes in the law, we can get the pricing flexibility we need and the latitude to bring new products to market faster . . . . Some say the solution is to privatize the Postal Service. Well that depends on what they mean. If it means putting for sale signs in our lobby windows and selling off the mail to the highest bidder, that's a bad idea. No private company accountable to Wall Street can carry out our national mandate. America needs the communications safety net that the Postal Service provides . . . . On the other hand, if they mean freeing the Postal Service to become more businesslike and market driven, we have something to talk about.[17]

If Congress and the Postal Rate Commission would grant the Postal Service such pricing power and freedom to enter new markets, the Postmaster General said, this traditionally nonprofit enterprise "could become a profit center for the federal

---

17. Address by Postmaster General Marvin Runyon to the National Press Club, Washington, D.C. (Jan. 31, 1995) (available in LEXIS News Library) [hereinafter *National Press Club Speech*].

government" and "out-deliver any competitor."[18] As we shall explore in this book, it is unclear what "profit" means for the Postal Service, because its statutory mandate is to break even,[19] but its actual experience in seventeen of the past twenty-three years has been that the enterprise has operated at a loss.[20]

The GAO's 1992 report looms prominently in the postmaster general's proposals. In March 1995 the new chairman of the House Subcommittee on the Postal Service wrote to the comptroller general, asking whether the GAO continued to adhere to the recommendations contained in its 1992 report to Congress.[21] Regardless of what the GAO might have thought about its 1992 report three years later, the Postal Service in April 1995 reaffirmed its position by petitioning the Postal Rate Commission to grant it the pricing flexibility recommended in the GAO's 1992 report.[22]

The Postal Service's drive to expand into other markets is merely a new manifestation of a long-established policy. The extension of the Post Office into parcel post service by Congress in 1912 had been the final result of forty years of debate and lobbying by a succession of postmasters general.[23] More recently the Postal Service unsuccessfully pursued entry into electronic mail. The Postal Service is contemplating ex-

---

18. *Id.*
19. 39 U.S.C. § 3621.
20. *Hearings Before the Subcomm. on the Postal Service of the House Comm. on Government Reform and Oversight*, 104th Cong., 1st Sess. (June 14, 1995) (testimony of James A. Rogers, Vice President, United Parcel Service).
21. Letter from John M. McHugh, Chairman, Subcommittee on the Postal Service, House Committee on Government Reform and Oversight, to Charles A. Bowsher, Comptroller General of the United States, United States General Accounting Office, Mar. 7, 1995 (copy on file with author).
22. Petition of United States Postal Service to Initiate Rulemaking, PRC Dkt. No. RM 95-4 (filed before the Postal Rate Commission, Apr. 10, 1995).
23. Edith M. Phelps, *Parcels Post, in* DEBATERS' HANDBOOK SERIES 1 (H.W. Wilson Co. 1913).

pansion into a host of new businesses, including overnight delivery of merchandise ordered through on-screen shopping from a central warehouse, electronic transmission of business reply mail, electronic mail certification for guaranteeing delivery, and providing access to the information superhighway in post offices.[24] In August 1995 the Postal Service announced that it would begin a year-long test of delivering unaddressed advertising circulars of the sort already delivered by newspapers and bulk mailers.[25] Are those activities appropriate and desirable for the Postal Service? Should a public enterprise compete with and possibly displace private business? Should the Postal Service be given the latitude to expand its range of products and services? Or, should public policy protect competition from the postal monopoly? Those are questions that have immediate relevance to other government businesses —such as Comsat and INTELSAT, to name only two—which compete against private telecommunications firms.[26]

Public ownership and control of postal services exist for historical reasons but constitute an important exception from most industries in the United States, which are privately owned and operated. It is now a propitious time to review the role of the government in postal services. Beginning in the mid-1970s, an ideological and electoral movement arose to reevaluate the functions of the state, including allocation of

---

24. *National Press Club Speech, supra* note 17.
25. Bill McAllister, *Special Delivery for 'Junk Mail'*, WASH. POST, Aug. 18, 1995, at A1; Asra Q. Nomani, *Newspaper, Direct-Mail Firms Blast Postal Service's New Plan for Fliers*, WALL ST. J., Aug. 21, 1995, at A2. In response to protests from private bulk mail delivery companies, the Postal Service announced less than a month later that it would postpone the test. *Postal Service Delays Test of New Bulk Mail Delivery*, WALL ST. J., Aug. 31, 1995, at A10.
26. *See* JOSEPH E. STIGLITZ, MARIUS SCHWARTZ & ERIC D. WOLFF, TOWARDS COMPETITION IN INTERNATIONAL SATELLITE SERVICES: RETHINKING THE ROLE OF INTELSAT (Council of Economic Advisers draft, June 1995).

income and resources, economic intervention in the economy, and the growth of government services. This movement began successful efforts to deregulate industry that resulted in the removal of government controls over some portions of transportation, telecommunications, energy, and securities brokerage. Consideration of government ownership and control over postal systems represents a return to basic precepts regarding the economic activities of the state.

The postal monopoly differs from the utility industries. Even though they are subject to some forms of federal, state, and municipal regulation, the utility industries in the United States traditionally are privately owned and operated. In the electric power industry, even though New Deal policies favored publicly provided power over investor-owned utilities, they did not represent a turning away from private enterprise. Congress established the Tennessee Valley Authority and the Bonneville Power Administration to provide subsidized hydroelectric power and to be a "yardstick" for private utilities.[27] At the same time, the (Wheeler-Rayburn) Public Utility Act of 1935 increased federal and state authority over privately owned companies.[28] The regulatory system erected over most of the twentieth century is now in the process of being dismantled and reorganized, especially with the proposed opening of telecommunications and electric power markets to competition.

The U.S. system of private companies contrasts with that of the social democracies of Europe, in which utility services such as electricity, telecommunications, and postal services routinely are provided by government-owned enterprises. The presumption in a market economy is that private enterprises should provide goods and services. Competition

---

27. LEONARD S. HYMAN, AMERICA'S ELECTRIC UTILITIES: PAST, PRESENT AND FUTURE 111 (Public Utilities Reports, Inc. 5th ed. 1994)

28. Titles I and II of the act were the Public Utility Holding Company Act (PUHCA) and the Federal Power Act (FPA).

between private companies yields cost efficiencies and innovation. There is substantial evidence that legally protected government monopolies often are sources of cost inefficiency, bureaucratic decision making, and obsolete technology.

There can be economic grounds for public provision of an essential or important service if policy makers can identify a market failure that prevents private provision of the service and can discern an important government advantage in providing the service. Proponents of the public Postal Service have failed to identify such a market failure. Postal services are far from being "public goods" because costs are sensitive to volumes, congestion externalities in production are present, and customer access can be easily excluded. Moreover, pricing of delivery services rations access to postal services, as it does with any privately provided product or service. The absence of market failure also is evident from the extensive services that private carriers of parcel post, express mail, and package delivery provide. The presence of multiple substitutes for public postal services—including telecommunications and facsimile, electronic mail, private carriers, and transportation— effectively mitigates any losses that might arise from some government advantage, however unlikely such an advantage may be.

The market failure that typically is used to justify public control of entry, though not necessarily public provision of a service, is that the market cannot achieve cost gains from natural monopoly. Our discussion demonstrates that, although there may be some economies of scale and scope in postal delivery services, those economies are far from sufficient to argue for a protected monopoly for the services. Even if there were such a monopoly, it could be privately owned, as are public utilities.

The same reasons that favor private over public provision of postal services apply to the question of whether the government should compete with the private sector for providing those services. If the private sector can provide the service, there is no role for government in the market as supplier. Moreover, when expansion of government provision of such services interferes with private provision, thus reducing opportunities for private concerns to recover their investments, government supply of postal services represents a taking of private property by interference with ongoing commercial concerns.

In this book we analyze on legal and economic grounds the proposition that the Postal Service should be granted greater flexibility to compete against private firms. In chapter 2 we describe the nature and extent of the Postal Service's legal monopoly. In chapter 3 we demonstrate why technological justifications for the postal monopoly are no longer valid. We show in chapter 4 that public provision of the full range of postal services is no longer needed. In chapter 5 we show that public control of the government's postal monopoly is necessary but so far has been ineffectual. We explain in chapter 6 that Postal Service pricing and regulations cause competitive problems for private firms because of incorrect measurement and misallocation of attributable costs and because of misuse of Ramsey-pricing principles.

We conclude, in chapter 7, by presenting the four options that Congress has to address the problem of protecting competition from the postal monopoly. The first is for Congress simply to acquiesce to the Postal Service's current pattern of empire building. The second is to privatize the Postal Service. The third is to commercialize the Postal Service, by which we mean turning the Postal Service into a publicly owned business free of any statutory privileges or burdens relative to private firms. The fourth is to retain the Private Express Statutes and all other statutory privileges and burdens, but to subject the Postal Service to far more rigorous public oversight and to explicit antitrust scrutiny. We conclude that, of those four, commercialization is the most attractive option because it is politically feasible and would appreciably enhance economic welfare.

2

The Nature and Extent of the Postal Monopoly

ARTICLE I OF THE CONSTITUTION empowers, but does not mandate, Congress "[t]o establish Post Offices and post Roads."[1] Nothing in this constitutional text requires Congress either to establish a public enterprise to deliver the mail or to create a monopoly over mail delivery.[2] Nonetheless, the Supreme Court long ago established that the "power possessed

---

1. U.S. CONST. art. I, § 8, cl. 7.
2. For insightful analyses of the history of the U.S. postal monopoly, see William Ty Mayton, *The Mission and Methods of the Postal Service*, in GOVERNING THE POSTAL SERVICE 60 (J. Gregory Sidak ed., AEI Press 1994); George L. Priest, *Socialism, Eastern Europe, and the Question of the Postal Monopoly*, in id. at 46, 54; George L. Priest, *The History of the Postal Monopoly in the United States*, 18 J.L. & ECON. 33 (1975). These authors extend Ronald Coase's critiques of the British postal monopoly. R. H. Coase, *The British Post Office and the Messenger Companies*, 4 J.L. & ECON. 12 (1961); R. H. Coase, *The Postal Monopoly in Great Britain: An Historical Survey*, in ECONOMIC ESSAYS IN COMMEMORATION OF THE DUNDEE SCHOOL OF ECONOMICS 1931-1955 at 25 (J. K. Eastham ed. 1955); R. H. Coase, *Rowland Hill and the Penny Post*, 6 ECONOMICA 423 (n.s. 1939).

by Congress embraces the regulation of the entire postal system of the country."[3] Rather than promote a competitive mail delivery industry, Congress chose to create and perpetuate through the Private Express Statutes a public enterprise with monopoly power. The courts have repeatedly upheld the Private Express Statutes in the face of constitutional challenges to the monopoly.[4]

Before one can understand the fallacy of the GAO's recommendations concerning inverse elasticity pricing, one must know the nature and extent of the postal monopoly under the Private Express Statutes. The postal monopoly is a combination of statutory law and regulation encompassing "letters" and the archaic and now-irrelevant term "packets." The definition of "letters" consequently is critical to understanding the extent to which the letter segments of first class and third class mail are closed to competition. The Postal Service defines a letter to be "a message directed to a specific person or address and recorded in or on a tangible object," although that definition is subject to a multitude of qualifications and caveats.[5] The result is unlike that in any other regulated industry: Because the Postal Service claims for itself the term "letter," which defines the extent of its monopoly, the monopolist has the power largely to define the scope of its own monopoly. Writing in 1974, John Haldi observed that "the one consistent thread running through" the "complex and conflicting interpretations of what constitutes a letter" is that "the Post Office

---

3. *Ex parte* Jackson, 96 U.S. (6 Otto) 727, 732 (1878).

4. Associated Third Class Mail Users *v.* United States Postal Serv., 600 F.2d 824 (D.C. Cir.), *cert. denied*, 444 U.S. 837 (1979); United States Postal Serv. *v.* Brennan, 574 F.2d 712 (2d Cir. 1978); United States *v.* Black, 569 F.2d 1111 (10th Cir. 1978); Williams *v.* Wells Fargo & Co. Express, 177 F. 352 (8th Cir. 1910); Blackham *v.* Gresham, 16 F. 609 (C.C.N.Y 1883); Associated Third Class Mail Users *v.* United States Postal Serv., 440 F. Supp. 1211 (D.D.C. 1977). *See also* United States *v.* Thompson, F. Cas. No. 16489 (D. Mass. 1846).

5. 39 C.F.R. § 310.1(a).

has construed the term so as to restrict competition and maximize its own revenues."[6] Thus, certain "nonletters"—such as bills, which constitute a substantial fraction of the mail stream—are construed to be letters. At the same time some kinds of letters are exempted from the Private Express Statutes and may be carried "out of mail." Nonetheless, Postal Service regulations may have the effect of dictating price floors for its private competitors, as is the case in overnight mail.

THE PRIVATE EXPRESS STATUTES

What is perhaps most notable about the Private Express Statutes is that their key provisions appear in the United States Criminal Code. Apart from all else that it is, the postal monopoly is the threat of criminal punishment. Section 1694 of Title 18 forbids the carriage of matter out of mail over post routes:

> Whoever, having charge or control of any conveyance operating by land, air, or water, which regularly performs trips at stated periods on any post route, or from one place to another between which the mail is regularly carried, carries, otherwise than in the mail, any letters or packets, except such as relate to some part of the cargo of such conveyance, or to the current business of the carrier, or to some article carried at the same time by the same conveyance, shall, except as otherwise provided by law, be fined under this title.[7]

---

6. JOHN HALDI, POSTAL MONOPOLY: AN ASSESSMENT OF THE PRIVATE EXPRESS STATUTES 13 (AEI Press 1974).

7. 18 U.S.C. § 1694.

An analogous provision, section 1695, forbids the carriage of matter out of mail on vessels and adds the threat of imprisonment.[8] Likewise, section 1693 makes the collection, receipt, or carriage of mail in contravention of the Private Express Statutes punishable by both fine and imprisonment.[9]

A more seriously punishable crime than the mere carriage of matter out of mail is the creation of a private express network capable of competing with the Postal Service. While sections 1693, 1694, and 1695 take aim at the labor and transportation inputs that would be directly used to provide competitive delivery of letters, section 1696 addresses the deployment of capital and managerial labor to establish a private express network:

> Whoever establishes any private express for the conveyance of letters or packets, or in any manner causes or provides for the conveyance of the same by regular trips or at stated periods over any post route which is or may be established by law, or from any city, town, or place to any other city, town, or place, between which the mail is regularly carried, shall be fined not more than $500 or imprisoned not more than six months, or both.[10]

---

8. "Whoever carries any letter or packet on board any vessel which carries the mail, otherwise than in such mail, shall, except as otherwise provided by law, be fined under this title or imprisoned not more than thirty days, or both." *Id.* § 1695.

9. "Whoever, being concerned in carrying the mail, collects, receives, or carries any letter or packet, contrary to law, shall be fined under this title or imprisoned not more than thirty days, or both." *Id.* § 1693.

10. *Id.* § 1696(a). Perhaps because this portion of section 1696(a) is so heavy-handed, the subsection continues with the following safe harbor that would seem obvious: "This section shall not prohibit any person from receiving and delivering to the nearest post office, postal car, or other authorized depository for mail matter any mail matter properly stamped." *Id.*

The Private Express Statutes do not merely punish entrepreneurs who establish or operate private express networks. Any *consumer* of a private express company in violation of section 1696 is subject to fine under a strict liability standard.[11] A person also is subject to fine if he knowingly transports a person who is acting as a private express.[12] Amplifying those statutory prohibitions on private express are numerous postal regulations, the broadest of which provides: "It is generally unlawful under the Private Express Statutes for any person other than the Postal Service in any manner to send or carry a letter on a post route or in any manner to cause or assist such activity. Violation may result in injunction, fine or imprisonment or both and payment of postage lost as a result of the illegal activity."[13]

Despite their relative obscurity—and perhaps as an indication of the strain being placed on the postal monopoly—the Private Express Statutes generated four Supreme Court decisions between 1981 and 1991.[14] Writing for the Court in *Air Courier Conference of America* v. *American Postal Workers Union*, Chief Justice Rehnquist described the Private

---

11. "Whoever transmits by private express or other unlawful means, or delivers to any agent thereof, or deposits at any appointed place, for the purpose of being so transmitted any letter or packet, shall be fined under this title." *Id.* § 1696(b).
12. "Whoever, having charge or control of any conveyance operating by land, air, or water, knowingly conveys or knowingly permits the conveyance of any person acting or employed as a private express for the conveyance of letters or packets, and actually in possession of the same for the purpose of conveying them contrary to law, shall be fined under this title." *Id.* § 1697.
13. 39 C.F.R. § 310.2.
14. Air Courier Conf. of Am. *v.* American Postal Workers Union, 498 U.S. 517 (1991); Regents of Univ. of Cal. *v.* Public Employment Relations Bd., 485 U.S. 589 (1988); Perry Education Ass'n *v.* Perry Local Educators' Ass'n, 460 U.S. 37 (1983); United States Postal Serv. *v.* Council of Greenburgh Civic Ass'ns, 453 U.S. 114 (1981) (construing 18 U.S.C. § 1725, which prohibits the deposit of unstamped "mailable matter" in a letterbox approved by the Postal Service).

Express Statutes as a classic attempt by government to prevent cream skimming in the name of preserving universal service at a (subsidized) uniform price:

> The monopoly was created by Congress as a revenue protection measure for the Postal Service to enable it to fulfill its mission. It prevents private competitors from offering service on low-cost routes at prices below those of the Postal Service, while leaving the Service with high-cost routes and insufficient means to fulfill its mandate of providing uniform rates and service to patrons in all areas, including those that are remote or less populated.[15]

Thus, the postal monopoly is yet another example of the most pervasive and contentious issue in regulated industries: the suppression of competitive entry to prevent cream skimming.[16]

Typically, a private firm subject to regulation has assumed "incumbent burdens" in return for the regulator's assurance that the firm will have the opportunity to earn a competitive return on, and recovery of, its invested capital, along with the compensation for the full cost of providing service.[17] The incumbent burdens usually include the obligation to provide universal service at a fixed price, regardless of the

---

15. 498 U.S. 517, 519 (1991) (citations omitted). *Accord*, Regents of Univ. of Cal. v. Public Employment Relations Bd., 485 U.S. 589, 598 (1988).

16. *See* 2 ALFRED E. KAHN, THE ECONOMICS OF REGULATION 220–46 (MIT Press rev. ed. 1988).

17. *See* WILLIAM J. BAUMOL & J. GREGORY SIDAK, TRANSMISSION PRICING AND STRANDED COSTS IN THE ELECTRIC POWER INDUSTRY 101–02 (AEI Press 1995); William J. Baumol & J. Gregory Sidak, *Stranded Costs*, 18 HARV. J.L. & PUB. POL'Y 835 (1995); Paul W. MacAvoy, Daniel F. Spulber & Bruce E. Stangle, *Is Competitive Entry Free?: Bypass and Partial Deregulation in Natural Gas Markets*, 6 YALE J. ON REG. 209, 210 (1989).

true cost of service. Chief Justice Rehnquist observed in *Air Courier Conference* that the legislative history from 1845 revealed that one of the two intended purposes of the Private Express Statutes was to ensure subsidized universal mail service:

> [I]t was thought to be the duty of the Government to serve outlying, frontier areas, even if it meant doing so below cost. Thus, the revenue protection provisions were not seen as an end in themselves, nor in any sense as a means of ensuring certain levels of public employment, but rather were seen as the means to achieve national integration and to ensure that all areas of the Nation were equally served by the Postal Service.[18]

New entrants into regulated markets, of course, first target the customers who are required by regulators to pay prices exceeding cost so that other customers may be charged prices below cost. Furthermore, new entrants may be able to avoid regulations that thwart the use of the least-cost production technology and in this sense may be more efficient producers than the incumbent. Again, as *Air Courier Conference* indicates, the Supreme Court subscribes to that view of the postal monopoly:

---

18. 498 U.S. at 527 (citation omitted). According to the Chief Justice, the second purpose for the Private Express Statutes was, surprisingly, to prevent arbitrage: "[T]he Postmaster General and the States most distant from the commercial centers of the Northeast believed that the postal monopoly was necessary to prevent users of faster private expresses from taking advantage of early market intelligence and news of international affairs that had not yet reached the general populace through the slower mails." *Id.* at 920 (citing S. DOC. NO. 66, 28th Cong., 2d Sess. 3-4 (1845)). The advent of ubiquitous, instantaneous, and inexpensive telecommunications makes this second justification for the statutory monopoly over letter mail obsolete.

> The Private Express Statutes enable the Postal Service to fulfill its responsibility to provide service to all communities at a uniform rate by preventing private courier services from competing selectively with the Postal Service on its most profitable routes. If competitors could serve the lower cost segment of the market, leaving the Postal Service to handle the high-cost services, the Service would lose lucrative portions of its business, thereby increasing its average unit cost and requiring higher prices to all users.[19]

As we shall show in chapters 4 and 5, this analysis requires some modification when applied to a publicly owned and controlled enterprise like the Postal Service. Nonetheless, the policy concerns offered to justify the Private Express Statutes are thoroughly familiar to anyone conversant in the economics of regulated industries.

THIRD CLASS MAIL AND THE PRIVATE EXPRESS STATUTES

The Private Express Statutes create the postal monopoly and set forth the conditions under which private persons may carry letters. But those statutes are singularly vague as to what mail comprises a "letter." Thus, the scope of the monopoly, enforceable by criminal sanction, is itself vague. The legislative and administrative histories of the Private Express Statutes do not cure the ambiguity, for they can be simultaneously cited to support both the broadest and narrowest possible interpretations of the scope of the Postal Service's monopoly.[20] This

---

19. *Id.*
20. *See* Associated Third Class Mail Users *v.* United States Postal Serv., 600 F.2d 824 (D.C. Cir. 1979) (Wright, J.).

The Nature and Extent of the Postal Monopoly 19

ambiguity is particularly manifest with respect to third class mail, which consists primarily of advertising circulars and handbills—mail material that does not intuitively fit the common conception of a letter.

The Postal Service considers a piece of third class mail to be a "letter" and thus within the postal monopoly created by the Private Express Statutes as long as it has an address marked on it. In *Associated Third Class Mail Users* v. *United States Postal Service*, the U.S. Court of Appeals for the District of Columbia Circuit agreed. The court acknowledged that the statutes, as well as their legislative and administrative histories, "belie any notion that a single definition of 'letter' flows ineluctably from materials at hand."[21] Nonetheless, the D.C. Circuit deferred to the Postal Service's broad test for defining a letter on the basis of "the presence or absence of an address."[22] The court concluded that "the Postal Service has settled upon a reasonable criterion," and "its definition suffers from no more than the level of arbitrariness which is inevitable."[23] Consequently, most third class mail is construed by law to be within the scope of the Postal Service's monopoly.

EXEMPTIONS FROM AND EXCEPTIONS TO THE PRIVATE EXPRESS STATUTES

The Private Express Statutes and the regulations interpreting them contain a number of exceptions that permit pockets of competition to develop for the delivery of certain kinds of letters.

Out of Mail Letters Bearing Postage

The Private Express Statutes provide a blanket exemption for

---

21. *Id.* at 827.
22. *Id.* at 830.
23. *Id.*

letters carried out of mail if the letter bears the full postage and conforms to certain other conditions. Section 601(a) of Title 39 provides: "A letter may be carried out of the mails when—

> (1) it is enclosed in an envelope;
>
> (2) the amount of postage which would have been charged on the letter if it had been sent by mail is paid by stamps, or postage meter stamps, on the envelope;
>
> (3) the envelope is properly addressed;
>
> (4) the envelope is so sealed that the letter cannot be taken from it without defacing the envelope;
>
> (5) any stamps on the envelope are canceled in ink by the sender; and
>
> (6) the date of the letter, of its transmission or receipt by the carrier is endorsed on the envelope in ink."[24]

As a matter of elementary economic theory, this provision is flawed because it overcompensates the Postal Service. The opportunity cost to the Postal Service from the delivery of a letter out of mail is the forgone contribution that the letter would make to recovering the Service's common fixed costs. The opportunity cost is *not* the full price of postage for that letter. The Postal Service, after all, avoids costs when out-of-mail delivery occurs, and cost avoidance is the very rationale

---

24. 39 U.S.C. § 601(a).

that the Postal Service offers in a different context when giving discounts for presorted mail and mail using ZIP+4 codes or bar codes.[25]

Overcompensating the Postal Service for its opportunity costs deters entry into the provision of end-to-end mail services for letters. That result is not surprising, of course. The purpose of the Private Express Statutes is to suppress competition, and they expressly prohibit the private provision of other critical inputs (such as carriage and receipt of letters out of mail) that would be necessary for a firm to compete against the Postal Service in end-to-end postal services for letters.

General Exceptions

There are five general exceptions to the statutory monopoly on letter mail: letters accompanying cargo, letters of the carrier, letters by private hands without compensation, letters by special messenger, and carriage of letters before or after mailing.[26]

Letters Accompanying Cargo. Section 1694's prohibition on the private carriage of mail excludes "letters or packets . . . [that] relate to some part of the cargo of such conveyance . . . or to some article carried at the same time by the same conveyance."[27] Accordingly, Postal Service regulations permit the sending or carrying of letters if they "accompany and relate in all substantial respects to some part of the cargo or to the ordering, shipping or delivering of the cargo."[28] A packing slip, for example, that is enclosed with a parcel that is being

---

25. *See, e.g.,* Postal Rate and Fee Changes, 1994, Dkt. No. R94-1, at V-10 to V-16 (Postal Rate Commission 1994).
26. 39 C.F.R. § 310.3.
27. 18 U.S.C. § 1694.
28. 39 C.F.R. § 310.3(a).

privately delivered need not be carried by the Postal Service. The necessity of such an exception on grounds of transactional efficiency is obvious.

Letters of the Carrier. Section 1694's prohibition on the private carriage of mail also excludes "letters or packets . . . [that] relate . . . to the current business of the carrier."[29] This proviso is known as the "letters of the carrier" exception to the Private Express Statutes.[30] The Postal Service has promulgated the following regulation to implement this exception:

> The sending or carrying of letters is permissible if they are sent by or addressed to the person carrying them. If the individual actually carrying the letters is not the person sending the letters or to whom the letters are addressed, then such individual must be an officer or employee of such person . . . and the letters must relate to the current business of such person.[31]

The letters of the carrier exception would, for example, permit United Airlines to carry on its aircraft interoffice letters relating to the "current business" of that company.

In *Regents of the University of California* v. *Public Employment Relations Board*, the Supreme Court considered whether, for purposes of section 1694, certain letters were

---

29. 18 U.S.C. § 1694.
30. *See* 39 C.F.R. § 310.3(b); Regents of the Univ. of Cal. *v.* Public Employment Relations Bd., 485 U.S. 589 (1988); Perry Ed. Ass'n *v.* Perry Local Educators' Ass'n, 460 U.S. 37 (1983); United States *v.* Erie R.R., 235 U.S. 513 (1915); Fort Wayne Community Schools *v.* Fort Wayne Ed. Ass'n, Inc., 977 F.2d 358 (7th Cir. 1992); *Letters Outside of the Mails Carried by Railroad Companies—Statutory Construction*, 21 Op. Att'y Gen. 394 (1886).
31. 39 C.F.R. § 310.3(b)(1).

related to the current business of the University of California.[32] A union attempting to organize the employees of the university tried to send them letters through the university's internal mail. When the university refused to deliver the letters, it was sued by the union. The Supreme Court held that the union's letters did not qualify for the letters of the carrier exception because they did not relate to the "current business" of the university; rather, the letters related to "the Union's efforts to organize certain of [the university's] employees into a bargaining unit," which, the Court said, "can be accurately described only as the Union's current business," not the university's.[33]

The letters of the carrier exception raises two interesting analytical problems. First, as *Regents of the University of California* demonstrates, the exception is a rule that turns on the content of the letter. Thus, it leads to relatively intrusive, fact-specific inquiries. Second, because the exception requires that the letter relate to the current business of the carrier, it expands with the scale and scope of the enterprise of which the carrier is a part.[34] Thus, two letters being transported from New York to Los Angeles, one by United Airlines and the other by American Airlines, could be treated differently under this exception depending on what the letters said and what the current lines of business of the two airlines happened to be at that moment.

---

32. 485 U.S. 589 (1988).
33. *Id*. at 594.
34. "Separately incorporated carriers are separate entities for purposes of this exception, regardless of any subsidiary, ownership, or leasing arrangement. When, however, two concerns jointly operate an enterprise with joint employees and share directly in its revenues and expenses, either of the concerns may carry the letters of the joint enterprise." 39 C.F.R. § 310.3(b)(3). *See also* United States v. Erie R.R., 235 U.S. 513 (1915).

Letters by Private Hands Without Compensation. Section 1696 contains an exemption for "the conveyance or transmission of letters or packets by private hands without compensation."[35] Although this statutory provision enables the Postal Service to state affirmatively in its regulations that the "sending or carrying of letters without compensation is permitted,"[36] the Postal Service is then compelled to specify at considerable length what constitutes "compensation." The Postal Service considers compensation to consist of not only "a monetary payment for services rendered," but also "non-monetary valuable consideration and . . . good will."[37]

Letters by Special Messenger. Section 1696 also exempts private carriage "by special messenger employed for the particular occasion only."[38] The Postal Service interprets that provision to permit the "use of a special messenger employed for the particular occasion only . . . to transmit letters if not more than twenty-five letters are involved," but the messenger service may only be used "on an infrequent, irregular basis by the sender or addressee of the message."[39] A special messenger is defined to be someone "who, at the request of either the sender or the addressee, picks up a letter from the sender's home or place of business and carries it to the addressee's home or place of business."[40] This exception permits, for example, the familiar phenomenon in any major

---

35. 39 U.S.C. § 1696(c).
36. 39 C.F.R. § 310.3(c).
37. *Id.* "Thus, for example, when a business relationship exists or is sought between the carrier and its user, carriage by the carrier of the user's letter will ordinarily not fall under this exception; or, when a person is engaged in the transportation of goods or persons for hire, his carrying of letters 'free of charge' for customers whom he does charge for the carriage of goods or persons does not fall under this exception." *Id.*
38. 39 U.S.C. § 1696(c).
39. 39 C.F.R. § 310.3(d)(1).
40. *Id.* § 310.3(d)(2).

city of bicycle couriers who speed time-sensitive documents from one business office to another.

By itself, however, the special messenger exemption is not so broad as to permit a private express company to engage in the aggregation of mail for distribution and delivery (as through a hub-and-spoke network, for example). A special messenger may not be "a messenger or carrier operating regularly between fixed points."[41] The creation of a hub and spokes would obviously entail regular carriage between fixed points. The special messenger exemption can therefore be viewed as constraining the efficiency of private express companies by denying them the opportunity to employ a network architecture of nodes and fixed links.

Carriage of Letters Before or After Mailing. The Postal Service permits the private carriage of letters "which enter the mail stream at some point between their origin and their destination."[42] So, for example, the Postal Service allows private firms to engage in

> the pickup and carriage of letters which are delivered to post offices for mailing; the pickup and carriage of letters at post offices for delivery to addressees; and the bulk shipment of individually addressed letters ultimately carried by the Postal Service.[43]

This exception to the Private Express Statutes makes it easier for the Postal Service to offer discounts for bulk mailing and presorting.[44] Without this exception, bulk mailing and

---

41. *Id.*
42. *Id.* § 310.3(e)(1).
43. *Id.* § 310.3(e)(2).
44. "The private carriage of letters from branches of an organization to a location for preparation for mailing does not constitute a consolidation. The

presorting could still be done *by the mailer*, and discounts could be given to that mailer; but mailers would not be able to employ bulk mailing and presorting bureaus to deliver mail to the Postal Service for the mailer.

Extremely Urgent Letters

The most significant exception to the Private Express Statutes (technically termed a "suspension" of the Statutes by the Postal Service) is for "extremely urgent letters."[45] Without that exception, Federal Express, United Parcel Service, and other private firms would be unable to compete in the express mail business. To be able to deliver extremely urgent letters, a private firm must satisfy either of two primary conditions, and then several secondary conditions of a more mechanical nature.

Primary Conditions. The Postal Service defines the primary, alternative conditions for private carriage of an extremely urgent letter in terms of (1) the timeliness of its delivery and (2) its absolute price or its price relative to first class mail.

Timeliness of Delivery. One criterion by which the Postal Service will suspend the Private Express Statutes for urgent letters is if "the value or usefulness of the letter would be lost or greatly diminished if it is not delivered within [the] time limits" specified in the Service's regulations.[46] The applicable time limits depend on the distance of the delivery:

> For letters dispatched within 50 miles of the intended destination, delivery of those dis-

---

private carriage of letters from an organization's point of mail delivery to its branches in the locality does not constitute a separation." *Id.* § 310.3(e)(3).
 45. 39 C.F.R. § 320.6.
 46. *Id.* § 320.6(b)(1).

patched by noon must be completed within 6 hours or by the close of the addressee's normal business hours that day, whichever is later, and delivery of those dispatched after noon and before midnight must be completed by 10 A.M. of the addressee's next business day. For other letters, delivery must be completed within 12 hours or by noon of the addressee's next business day.[47]

Those time limits do not apply to locations outside the forty-eight contiguous states.[48] The time limits do apply, however, "to letters dispatched and delivered wholly within Alaska, Hawaii, Puerto Rico or a territory or possession of the United States."[49]

The Postal Service has said, and at least one court has agreed, that, even if the time limits are met, the exception for extremely urgent letters does not apply if the value of the letter does not depend on meeting the time limit.[50]

Absolute or Relative Price. Price is the second, alternative criterion by which the Postal Service will determine whether to suspend the Private Express Statutes with respect to extremely urgent letters. The Postal Service will conclusively presume a letter to be extremely urgent, and thus exempt its private carriage from the Private Express Statutes, "if the amount paid for private carriage of the letter is at least three dollars or twice the applicable U.S. postage for First-Class Mail (including priority mail) whichever is the great-

---

47. *Id.*
48. *Id.* § 320.6(b)(3).
49. *Id.*
50. United States Postal Serv. *v.* O'Brien, 644 F. Supp. 140 (D.D.C. 1986).

er."[51]

As a practical business matter, this price test has become the operative standard for establishing that a letter is extremely urgent mail eligible for delivery by private carriers. That is so since the price test, unlike the test of timeliness of delivery, enables the private carrier to offer mailers the choice of next-day delivery in either the morning or afternoon, without regard to the letter's destination. Of course, one practical effect of the price test is that the Postal Service thereby sets a floor for the prices that its private competitors may charge for overnight mail.

Secondary Conditions. The secondary requirements for private carriage of extremely urgent letters are more mechanical. Nonetheless, those additional requirements provide insights into why companies like Federal Express and United Parcel Service conduct business in the way they do. The first such requirement concerns labeling:

> The sender must prominently mark the outside covers or containers of letters carried under this suspension with the words "Extremely Urgent" or "Private Carriage Authorized by Postal Regulations (39 CFR 320.6)" or with a similar legend identifying the letters as carried pursuant to this suspension [of the Private Express Statutes].[52]

It is surely because of that regulatory categorization, and not because of any inherent marketing value in the form of the label, that a Next Day Air letter of United Parcel Service states across the front, "EXTREMELY URGENT—Notify

---

51. 39 C.F.R. § 320.6(c).
52. *Id.* § 320.6(d).

addressee immediately upon receipt," and that a FedEx letter similarly states, "Extremely urgent: Recipient please hand deliver to addressee."

A second requirement is that each outside container or cover must show the name and address of the carrier and the addressee.[53] This requirement assists the Postal Service in policing its timeliness-by-distance test and reiterates a statutory requirement.[54]

A third requirement concerns the recording of the delivery time. The carrier's record "must be sufficient to show that the delivery of the letters was completed within the applicable time limitations, if carried under the authority of [timeliness of delivery], and must be made available for inspection at the request of the Postal Service."[55] This requirement explains why, apart from their desire to have continuous tracking of letters because customers value such service, Federal Express and United Parcel Service require their employees to record the time that an extremely urgent letter is delivered.

Penalties for Violating the Terms of Suspension. Postal Service regulations provide: "Upon discovery of activity made unlawful by the Private Express Statutes, the Postal Service may require any person or persons who engage in, cause, or assist such activity to pay an amount or amounts not exceeding the total postage to which it would have been entitled had it carried the letters between their origin and destination."[56] Moreover, if a private express company violates the terms of

---

53. *Id.*
54. 39 U.S.C. § 601.
55. 39 C.F.R. § 320.6(d). "The required records may be either in the form of notations on the containers or covers of any letters asserted to be carried under this suspension, or in the form of records kept by employees of the actual times they pick up and deliver such materials." *Id.*
56. *Id.* § 310.5(a).

the Postal Service's suspension of the Private Express Statutes for extremely urgent mail, the penalty may be "administrative revocation of the suspension as to such shipper or carrier for a period of one year" following a proceeding before a judicial officer of the Postal Service.[57] The judicial officer may reduce or extend the period of the revocation by not more than one year, "depending on such mitigating or aggravating factors as the extent of the postal revenue lost because of the violation and the presence or absence of good faith error or of previous violations."[58] In other words, the judicial officer really has the authority to revoke the suspension for up to twenty-four months. Furthermore, a revocation of the suspension "shall in no way limit other actions as to such shipper or carrier to enforce the Private Express Statutes by administrative proceedings for collection of postage . . . or by civil or criminal proceedings."[59]

For reasons that we shall explain presently, this administrative procedure for revoking the suspension of the Private Express Statutes for extremely urgent mail can provide the Postal Service powerful leverage over private express companies and their customers:

> The failure of a shipper or carrier to cooperate with an authorized inspection or audit conducted by the Postal Inspection Service for the purpose of determining compliance with the terms of this suspension *shall be deemed to create a presumption of a violation . . . and shall shift to the shipper or carrier the burden of establishing the fact of compliance.*[60]

---

57. *Id.* § 320.6(e).
58. *Id.*
59. *Id.*
60. *Id.* (emphasis added).

Because a judicial officer of the Postal Service—rather than an Article III judge or even an independent administrative law judge—is the person deciding the revocation proceeding, the Postal Service can, at will, raise the expected losses of such litigation for the shipper or carrier by asserting that the firm has failed to be sufficiently cooperative with inspectors, thereby shifting the burden of proof from the Postal Service to the firm. The significance of that threat becomes clearer as we next examine how the Postal Service has recently exercised its statutory powers of search and seizure with respect to the overnight letter services of private express companies—and the customers of such services.

ENFORCEMENT OF THE PRIVATE EXPRESS STATUTES BY THE POSTAL SERVICE

To enforce the Private Express Statutes, the Postal Service has used its powers of search and seizure against large mailers in both the private and public sectors. In a highly publicized incident in 1993, armed postal inspectors arrived at the Atlanta headquarters of Equifax Inc., a large credit reporting company, and demanded to know whether all the mail that it had sent by Federal Express was truly urgent, as required by the Postal Service's suspension of the Private Express Statutes for extremely urgent letters.[61] The inspectors asked why Equifax was not sending paychecks to outlying offices by regular mail, and they wanted to open personal mail. Equifax agreed to pay the Postal Service a penalty of $30,000, which the *Los Angeles Times* described as "essentially a fee allowing the firm to use Federal Express as it wished for the following year without Postal Service harassment."[62] From 1991 through 1994,

---

61. Bill McAllister, *Must It Get There Overnight?*, WASH. POST, Jan. 12, 1994, at A17.
62. Michael A. Hiltzik, *Postal Agency Faces Fight with High-Tech Rivals*, L.A. TIMES, Dec. 16, 1994, at A1.

the Postal Service reportedly collected $521,000 from twenty-one mailers following similar audits.[63] In addition, the Postal Service began investigating federal agencies' use of private overnight mail after discovering that the General Services Administration had negotiated with Federal Express to have overnight mail delivered for $3.75—compared with the Postal Service's overnight rate of $9.95 and Federal Express's standard rate of $15.50.[64]

The Postal Service's investigations of large mailers incensed members of Congress. Senator Paul Coverdell of Georgia introduced an amendment to the National Competitiveness Act asking the Postal Service to suspend further audits and fines temporarily until the GAO completed a study on the impact of permanently suspending such enforcement activity.[65] He also introduced a bill that would prohibit the Postal Service from fining or otherwise penalizing businesses that used private carriers to deliver letters that those businesses deemed to be urgent.[66] The Senate passed Senator Coverdell's resolution unanimously.[67] Thereafter, Postmaster General Runyon agreed not to use postal inspectors to audit

---

63. Eugene Makovic, *Time for Postal Competition*, ST. LOUIS POST-DISPATCH, July 21, 1994, at 7B. *See also* Paul Houston & Robert Shogan, *Washington Insight*, L.A. TIMES, Apr. 4, 1994, at A5 ("In the last five years, postal inspectors have marched into 41 businesses and collected more than $1 million in 'postage due' from companies that allegedly sent non-urgent mail by express service.").

64. *Private Couriers and Postal Service Slug It Out*, N.Y. TIMES, Feb. 14, 1994, at D1; *Post Office Sending Agencies a Message*, CHI. TRIBUNE, Jan. 16, 1994, at 10 ("The [Postal Service's audit] report noted that between 1990 and 1992 the Energy Department sent 423,635 items via private overnight services.").

65. 140 CONG. REC. S2589 (daily ed. Feb. 22, 1994) (amendment no. 1481).

66. Postal Fairness Act, S. 1541, 103d Cong., 1st Sess. (1993). Representative Fred Upton of Michigan introduced a similar bill in the House. H.R. 3796, 103d Cong., 2d Sess. (1994).

67. 140 CONG. REC. S3182, S3197 (daily ed. Mar. 17, 1994).

The Nature and Extent of the Postal Monopoly 33

customer mailings because, the *Washington Post* reported, the "bad publicity over the raids was not worth the small amount of postage the inspectors were collecting."[68]

THE REGULATION OF MAILBOXES

The mailbox is to the postal monopoly what the customer's telephone was to the former Bell System. The mailbox is the customer premises equipment. Just as the Bell System assiduously fought, starting with the *Hush-A-Phone* case, any attempt by the customer to attach unapproved devices to his telephone (which is to say, devices not manufactured by the Bell System's own Western Electric),[69] so also the Postal Service regulates what the customer may do with his own mailbox. The Postal Service's behavior is actually more overreaching than that of the monolithic Bell System in its heyday because the mailbox is clearly the customer's private property, whereas before the AT&T divestiture the customer merely leased his telephone from the Bell System.

Section 1725 of the Criminal Code prohibits the deposit of unstamped "mailable matter" in a customer letterbox approved by the Postal Service, and violations are subject to a fine.[70] In turn, the *Domestic Mail Manual*, which is incorpo-

---

68. Bill McAllister, *Postal Service Drops Promise on 2-Day Mail; Runyon Also Orders Halt to Raiding of Businesses*, WASH. POST, Mar. 25, 1994, at A21.

69. Hush-A-Phone Corp. v. United States, 238 F.2d 266 (D.C. Cir. 1956). *See* MICHAEL K. KELLOGG, JOHN THORNE & PETER W. HUBER, FEDERAL TELECOMMUNICATIONS LAW 171–75, 494–95, 499–502 (Little, Brown & Co. 1992) (discussing *Hush-A-Phone* and other "foreign attachment" cases).

70. "Whoever knowingly and willfully deposits any mailable matter such as statements of accounts, circulars, sale bills, or other like matter, on which no postage has been paid, in any letter box established, approved, or accepted by the Postal Service for the receipt or delivery of mail matter on any mail route with intent to avoid payment of lawful postage thereon, shall for each

rated by reference into Title 39 of the Code of Federal Regulations,[71] specifies the size, shape, and dimensions of mail receptacles.[72] The Postal Service requires that letterboxes and other receptacles designated for the delivery of mail "shall be used *exclusively* for matter which bears postage."[73]

The Postal Service's monopoly over mailbox access has three significant economic consequences. First, it enables the Postal Service to raise the cost of its rivals' deliveries: Federal Express or United Parcel Service, for example, may not leave its overnight letter in the mailbox if the recipient is not home. Unless the sender designates that the urgent letter may be left at the door if the recipient is not there, the carrier will have to attempt another delivery. A second and related consequence is to deter vertical integration into mail delivery by businesses (such as banks and utilities) with large numbers of routine mailings to virtually every postal customer on a given route. Congress did not enact section 1725 in 1845 as part of the original Private Express Statutes, but rather in 1934 to counteract vertical integration by such businesses into the delivery of bills:

> Business concerns, particularly utility companies, have within the last few years adopted the practice of having their circulars, statements of account, etc., delivered by private messenger, and have used as receptacles the letter boxes erected for the purpose of holding mail matter and approved by the Post Office Department for such purpose. This practice is depriving the Post Office Department of considerable revenue

---

such offense be fined not more than $300." 18 U.S.C. § 1725.

71. 39 C.F.R. pt. 3.

72. DOMESTIC MAIL MANUAL §§ 155.41, 155.43, 156.311, 156.51, 156.54.

73. *Id.* § 151.2 (emphasis added).

on matter which would otherwise go through the mails, and at the same time is resulting in the stuffing of letter boxes with extraneous matter.[74]

The third competitive consequence of section 1725 is that it raises the cost to the customer of substituting alternative delivery services for those of the Postal Service because his reliance on the former will require him to construct a new receptacle for private express deliveries.

In 1981 the Supreme Court considered in *United States Postal Service v. Council of Greenburgh Civic Associations* whether section 1725 violated the First Amendment on the grounds that a mailbox is a "public forum."[75] Government may regulate the time, manner, and place of speech conducted in a public forum, but speakers may not be excluded entirely from the public forum.[76] In the course of deciding this constitutional question with respect to mailboxes in *Greenburgh,* the Court construed section 1725 in a way that has significant consequences for the growth of competitive postal services.

In *Greenburgh,* the local postmaster notified a civic association that its practice of delivering messages to residents by placing unstamped notices in the letterboxes of private homes violated section 1725 and that, if the association persisted, it could be fined. The association then sued the Postal Service for declaratory and injunctive relief, contending that the enforcement of section 1725 would inhibit the association's communications with local residents and deny them the freedom of speech and press secured by the First Amend-

---

74. H.R. REP. NO. 709, 73d Cong., 2d Sess. 1 (1934); S. REP. NO. 742, 73d Cong., 2d Sess. 1 (1934).

75. 453 U.S. 114 (1981).

76. *See* Lillian R. BeVier, *Rehabilitating the Public Forum Doctrine: In Defense of Categories,* 1994 SUP. CT. REV. 79.

ment.[77]

The Supreme Court upheld section 1725 in *Greenburgh,* holding that the statute was neutral with respect to the content of the message sought to be placed in the mailbox.[78] Associate Justice Rehnquist then presented a puzzling rationale for the majority's view that a citizen has limited rights to offer access to his own mailbox:

> Nothing in any of the legislation or regulations recited above requires any person to become a postal customer. Anyone is free to live in any part of the country without having letters or packages delivered or received by the Postal Service by simply failing to provide the receptacle for those letters and packages which the statutes and regulations require. Indeed, the provision for "General Delivery" in most post offices enables a person to take advantage of the facilities of the Postal Service without ever having provided a receptacle at or near his premises conforming to the regulations of the Postal Service. What the legislation and regulations do require is that those persons who do wish to receive and deposit their mail at their home or business do so under the direction and control of the Postal Service.[79]

This reasoning is unpersuasive. The Court, having explained on one page why Congress considered universal mail service to be so essential in binding the republic together as to justify the creation of a public monopoly,[80] a few pages later feigns

---

77. 453 U.S. at 116-20.
78. *Id.* at 127.
79. *Id.* at 125-26.
80. *Id.* at 122.

indifference about the prospect of a nation of hermits who decline "to become . . . postal customer[s]."

The Court then followed this argument with the strained assertion that a quid pro quo had taken place, whereby the postal customer conveyed control over his mailbox to the Postal Service in return for the privilege of subjecting himself to its monopoly over letter mail:

> What is at issue in this case is solely the constitutionality of an Act of Congress which makes it unlawful for persons to use, without payment of a fee, a letterbox which has been designated an "authorized depository" of the mail by the Postal Service. As has been previously explained, when a letterbox is so designated, it becomes an essential part of the Postal Service's nationwide system for the delivery and receipt of mail. In effect, the postal customer, although he pays for the physical components of the "authorized depository," agrees to abide by the Postal Service's regulations in exchange for the Postal Service agreeing to deliver and pick up his mail.[81]

In all of its conjectures on the implicit contract between the citizen and the state, the Court evidently did not consider that some consumers might be willing to pay a higher price for the services of the Postal Service if they could keep the right to offer private express companies (or simply the local electric utility) access to their mailboxes. Although all the collected Private Express Statutes may be criticized for causing the allocative inefficiency and dynamic losses in innovation that economic analysis associates with statutory monopoly, none

---

81. *Id.* at 128.

matches the arrogance of section 1725 in its reliance on facile arguments to imply that consumers have willingly consented to the government's monopolization of their own property. *Greenburgh* invites the question, evidently not raised in the case, whether the federal government would be liable under the Takings Clause of the Fifth Amendment for the diminution of the value of the customer's mailbox caused by the Private Express Statutes.[82]

Conclusion

The Private Express Statutes are truly extraordinary in the history of American regulation of industry in the manner in which they grant and perpetuate monopoly power. The Postal Service does not passively reap the benefits of a monopoly conferred upon it by Congress. To the contrary, the Postal Service enjoys the power to expand the boundaries of that monopoly through the promulgation of its own regulations; the power to prosecute alleged violations of the monopoly through its own searches and seizures and its own enforcement actions for postage due; and the power to adjudicate alleged violations of the monopoly. In short, the Postal Service simultaneously exercises legislative, prosecutorial, and adjudicatory functions to circumscribe the private delivery of mail. Even at its apex, the Bell System could never take such liberties with the welfare of American consumers.

---

82. U.S. CONST. amend. V.

3

Technological Justifications for the Postal Monopoly

WE TURN NOW to the two main technological justifications offered for the protection and extension of the government's postal monopoly: (1) the presence of a natural monopoly production technology and (2) the existence of economies of scope. These arguments are used to imply that the monopoly over first class mail should be protected by statute and that the Postal Service should expand into other markets to achieve cost efficiencies. But why should there be this presumption of natural monopoly? The burden of proof should be on those asserting the existence of natural monopoly to show that it in fact exists, for it is an extreme proposition to say that the entire market for postal services is best served by a single firm. This placement of the burden of proof is especially appropriate if proponents of natural monopoly seek to preserve a statutory monopoly as well.

We show that the natural monopoly justification for the Postal Service's monopoly over letter mail is inconsistent with current technological and market developments in communications, delivery, and transportation services in the United

States. There is, consequently, no reason to conclude that postal delivery is a natural monopoly or to continue or extend the statutory monopoly on postal services. For similar reasons, the rationale based on economies of scope is also unpersuasive.

THE NATURAL MONOPOLY JUSTIFICATION FOR THE PUBLIC POSTAL MONOPOLY

The natural monopoly argument for public provision of postal services under a statutory monopoly has two components. First, the argument asserts that the provision of postal services is a natural monopoly. Second, the argument asserts that the cost savings from having a single provider of those services can only be achieved by regulatory exclusion of private competitors. Both assertions are incorrect.

We shall show that, given existing technology and market alternatives, the Postal Service is far from being a natural monopoly. Such technological arguments therefore cannot justify barring entry into the market because competitive, privately owned companies can realize the benefits of any increasing returns to scale that might inhere in the provision of postal services.

THE DEFINITION OF NATURAL MONOPOLY

A given production technology is said to exhibit the property of *natural monopoly* if a single firm can supply the market at lower cost than can two or more firms.[1] This textbook defini-

---

1. *See* DENNIS W. CARLTON & JEFFREY M. PERLOFF, MODERN INDUSTRIAL ORGANIZATION 295–96 (Harper Collins 2d ed. 1994); KENNETH E. TRAIN, OPTIMAL REGULATION: THE ECONOMIC THEORY OF NATURAL MONOPOLY 6–8 (MIT Press 1991); DANIEL F. SPULBER, REGULATION AND MARKETS 3 (MIT Press 1989); ROGER SHERMAN, THE REGULATION OF MONOPOLY 80–81 (Cambridge University Press 1989); SANFORD V. BERG &

tion of natural monopoly is based on a cost function that assigns total costs to outputs. The cost function has the natural monopoly property if a firm with that cost function has lower costs than would an allocation of output among two or more firms *using the same cost function*. If the technology of mail delivery exhibits natural monopoly characteristics, then a single firm can construct and operate that network at a lower cost than can two or more firms. Under those circumstances, the single firm is said to have *subadditive costs*.

The notion of natural monopoly is used as a justification for public ownership and control of the Postal Service and for the statutory monopoly over letter mail. According to that argument, regulation of entry is necessary to achieve static efficiency by establishing the least-cost industry structure—namely, a single firm.

One would expect under quite general conditions that competitive industries achieve the requisite cost efficiencies from consolidation of production, whether through expansion, mergers, or procurement contracts. It bears emphasis, however, that even if the Postal Service had subadditive costs, it would not follow that the Private Express Statutes are necessary unless one could show that the Postal Service is an *unsustainable* natural monopoly. The sustainability issue need not detain us. Even if there were cost efficiencies from natural monopoly, one would have to show that achieving those gains through a protected monopoly yielded benefits exceeding those from greater innovation, product variety, and lower administrative costs in a competitive market.

A number of important aspects of the definition of

JOHN TSCHIRHART, NATURAL MONOPOLY REGULATION: PRINCIPLES AND PRACTICE 22 (Cambridge University Press 1988); JEAN TIROLE, THE THEORY OF INDUSTRIAL ORGANIZATION 19-20 (MIT Press 1988); WILLIAM J. BAUMOL, JOHN C. PANZAR & ROBERT D. WILLIG, CONTESTABLE MARKETS AND THE THEORY OF INDUSTRY STRUCTURE 9 (Harcourt Brace Jovanovich 1982; rev. ed. 1988).

natural monopoly deserve emphasis, because understanding their implications is necessary for the correct application of the definition to mail delivery. The definition of natural monopoly begins with a *known technology*, as represented by the natural monopoly cost function. To assert that an industry is characterized by natural monopoly, one implicitly assumes that there is a single "best" technology that is commonly known, that all firms would have access to that technology, and that all firms operating that technology would be at the efficient production-possibility frontier.[2] In particular, the natural monopoly cost function is a long-run cost function, so that investment can be adjusted to achieve the efficient level of capital investment required for operating at minimum cost for each output level. In evaluating the applicability of the natural monopoly argument, we shall consider the extent to which those aspects of the definition of natural monopoly are indeed appropriate to the network of today's Postal Service.

On the basis of the standard definition, a cost function for a given production technology has the natural monopoly property if the technology exhibits *economies of scale* over the relevant range of output. In particular, economies of scale are said to be present if the marginal cost of production is less than the average cost of production over the relevant range of output.[3] Stated differently, economies of scale are said to exist over the relevant range of output when unit costs decline with the volume of production. Economies of scale are a sufficient condition for natural monopoly for a single-product firm.

Economies of scale can be due to many different technological factors. *Fixed costs* are a source of economies of scale that is particularly significant to industries that require physical networks, such as telecommunications, railroads, oil and natural gas pipelines, electricity, and water services.

2. SPULBER, *supra* note 1, at 138.
3. *Id.* at 115–18; CARLTON & PERLOFF, *supra* note 1, at 58–63.

Fixed costs are costs that do not vary with fluctuations in output, unlike operating or "variable" costs. The fixed costs of establishing a network system are the costs of facilities such as transmission lines, which are not sensitive to the level of transmission on the lines.

The need to avoid *duplication of facilities*, particularly duplication of the fixed costs of the network system, is an important component of the natural monopoly argument for regulation of mail delivery. The argument is that, because costs are minimized by not duplicating network infrastructure, regulators should bar the entry of competing carriers. This argument has been put forward in a wide range of regulated industries in which transmission or transportation facilities are a significant portion of total costs. We shall demonstrate that the duplication argument is inapplicable to mail delivery.

Is the Postal Service a Natural Monopoly?

The Postal Service is a wholesale and retail provider of delivery services. Those services involve three main components: (1) contracting for long-distance transportation, (2) regional sortation and transportation, and (3) local pickup, sortation, and delivery. There is no reason to presume that the technology for any of these components, whether taken singly or together, exhibits the properties of a natural monopoly.

Contracting for Long-Distance Transportation

Contracting for long-distance transportation is not a natural monopoly. Contracting for private transportation services dates to colonial times. In 1794 Congress authorized the Post Office to contract with private stagecoach lines, and later with steamships.[4] Today, the Postal Service predominantly relies on competitive providers of transportation, including airlines, trucks, ships, and railroads for long-distance transportation.[5] Its expenditures on the contractual transportation of mail in fiscal year 1994 were $3.33 billion.[6]

Clearly, contracting for such transportation does not exhibit natural monopoly properties. Without question, private firms are equally capable of procuring such services. Given the complexity of Postal Service procurement procedures, one would expect private companies to be able to do so at a cost lower than the Postal Service's. Indeed, the transportation companies themselves are able to coordinate the transportation services. Important developments in electronic data interchange and computerized reservation systems have drastically improved the efficiency of freight transportation. Those efficiencies are widely exploited by private companies and extend easily to transportation of mail, packages, and freight containers currently handled by the postal system.[7]

Regional Sortation and Transportation

Regional sortation and transportation also are not natural monopolies. Transportation by truck does not exhibit any natural monopoly properties. Although there may be organizational economies in coordinating and operating transportation

---

4. WAYNE E. FULLER, THE AMERICAN MAIL: ENLARGER OF THE COMMON LIFE 150 (University of Chicago Press 1972).

5. U.S. POSTAL SERVICE, COMPREHENSIVE STATEMENT ON POSTAL OPERATIONS, FY 1994, at 13 (1995) [hereinafter 1994 COMPREHENSIVE STATEMENT].

6. *Id.* The Postal Service nonetheless has its own fleet of twenty-nine aircraft and "operates the Eagle Hub in Indianapolis to supplement the air transportation of mail" to forty-six cities each night. *Id.* "Ninety percent of Express Mail that moves by air is routed through the Eagle Hub." *Id.*

7. "Virtually every piece of mail processed by the Postal Service is handled in a tray, sack, pallet, or rolling container." *Id.* at 15.

systems, regional transportation can be provided by multiple carriers. Certainly no one would suggest that a region be served by a single trucking company.

Regional sortation is not a natural monopoly either. Although there may be substantial economies of scale at the level of the individual sorting plant, this does not imply that a single company should operate all of the sorting plants across the country, or even within a region. The technology of regional sortation differs little from warehousing by wholesalers or retail chains for general merchandise, such as Safeway or Wal-Mart. No one would seriously suggest that wholesale supply of general merchandise be provided by a single company. In short, the notion that regional sortation and delivery have natural monopoly properties is not defensible.

Local Collection, Sortation, and Delivery

If there is no naturally monopolistic production technology for regional sortation and transportation or for long-distance transportation, then the Postal Service can be a natural monopoly only if local collection, sortation, and delivery exhibit characteristics of natural monopoly and do so in sufficient magnitude to dominate the constant or decreasing returns to scale found in regional sortation and transportation and in long-distance transportation.[8] Several economists have argued that economies of scale exist in the local delivery of mail.[9]

---

8. *See* George J. Stigler, *The Division of Labor Is Limited by the Extent of the Market*, 59 J. POL. ECON. 185 (1951), *reprinted in* GEORGE J. STIGLER, THE ORGANIZATION OF INDUSTRY 129 (Richard D. Irwin, Inc. 1968).

9. *See* John C. Panzar, *The Economics of Mail Delivery, in* GOVERNING THE POSTAL SERVICE 1, 2–3 (J. Gregory Sidak ed., AEI Press 1994); Cathy M. Rogerson & William M. Takis, *Economies of Scale and Scope and Competition in Postal Services, in* REGULATION AND THE NATURE OF POSTAL DELIVERY SERVICES 109, 113–15 (Michael A. Crew & Paul R. Kleindorfer eds., Kluwer Academic Publishers 1992); John C. Panzar, *Competition, Efficiency, and the Vertical Structure of Postal Services, in id.* at 91, 94; John

We shall show that such economies are limited in nature and do not suggest the need for entry restrictions into letter mail or government control of the Postal Service. Even the existence of such economies would not be sufficient evidence from which to conclude that a single firm should control all local service throughout the United States; rather, such economies would at most imply that each locality should have a single service provider.[10]

Moreover, the existence of local economies of scale would not justify unified control of the other two components of the Postal Service—regional sortation and transportation, and contracting for long-distance transportation. Even if there were vertical economies from combining local service with regional sortation and delivery, that condition would not justify horizontal integration across all localities; rather, it would support the creation of multiple vertical networks. Such a development would be roughly analogous to the growth of competing full-service networks in telecommunications.[11]

Network externalities are said to exist if adding more

C. Panzar, *Is Postal Service a Natural Monopoly?*, in COMPETITION AND INNOVATION IN POSTAL SERVICES 219, 223 (Michael A. Crew & Paul R. Kleindorfer eds., Kluwer Academic Publishers 1991); Bruce M. Owen & Robert D. Willig, *Economics and Postal Pricing*, in THE FUTURE OF THE POSTAL SERVICE 227, 236 (Joel L. Fleishman ed., Aspen Institute & Praeger Publishers 1983). *See also* MICHAEL A. CREW & PAUL R. KLEINDORFER, THE ECONOMICS OF POSTAL SERVICE 17-18 (Kluwer Academic Publishers 1992).

10. Sharon Oster has proposed that the Postal Service be divided into regional firms akin to the seven regional Bell operating companies formed by the AT&T breakup. Sharon M. Oster, *The Postal Service as a Public Enterprise*, in GOVERNING THE POSTAL SERVICE, *supra* note 9, at 31; Sharon M. Oster, *The Failure of Postal Reform*, 4 HUME PAPERS ON PUB. POL'Y (forthcoming 1995).

11. *See, e.g.*, WILLIAM J. BAUMOL & J. GREGORY SIDAK, TOWARD COMPETITION IN LOCAL TELEPHONY 10-19 (MIT Press & AEI Press 1994); J. Gregory Sidak, *Telecommunications in Jericho*, 81 CAL. L. REV. 1209, 1223-27 (1993).

customers or points of access to a network increases benefits or lowers costs to the existing customers of the network. Thus, telephone subscribers benefit from companies' hooking up additional customers because they can reach or be reached by more people. Even if network economies are present, this need not imply that there should be only one network operator and owner. Networking benefits can be achieved by interconnecting multiple networks. Moreover, portions of any given network can be owned and operated independently, with interconnections achieved through contracts. The analogy between postal networks and telecommunications, rail, and electric power networks is a tenuous one in any case. The local postal network bears little resemblance to those networks, because there are no location-specific transmission or rail lines that require capital investment. The postal routes covered by persons can be duplicated with relatively low capital expenditures.

The postal network may exhibit coordination economies in a particular form, as evidenced by the use of hub-and-spoke systems by competing private carriers. Such a pattern does not imply that only one network should operate, nor does it suggest that the government must own and operate such a network. Moreover, the coordination problems differ little from those of any transportation or wholesale company that must sort and route packages from one address to another. Those are routine functions that are effectively carried out by private companies. The coordination problems required for reliability by telecommunications or electricity networks are much more complex, require far more rapid responses, and have more severe consequences. Yet, even in those types of networks, coordination is achieved through contractual agreements and cooperation councils extending across individual companies.

Local service has three components: inward sortation by postal carriers, door-to-door delivery by postal carriers in trucks and on foot, and collection of mail at mailboxes and post offices. Those three elements involve well-understood, traditional technology. Economies of scale in those activities are minimal. The productive inputs involved, primarily labor services and vehicles, can be "smoothly" adjusted to reflect the volume of mail.

Inward Sortation. The inward sortation function can be split among multiple firms without a loss in efficiency. Just as inward sortation is split across postal employees, it can be split across companies. Indeed, larger mailers perform a degree of inward sortation to qualify for presort discounts.[12] Private firms, such as Mail Boxes Etc., that collect and forward mail also perform inward sortation in the sense of routing parcels to the fastest and least expensive carrier.[13] There are no apparent economies of scale of any significance for inward sortation.

Door-to-Door Delivery. The traditional natural monopoly argument emphasizes door-to-door delivery by postal carriers in trucks and on foot. In 1848 John Stuart Mill suggested the need to avoid duplication of effort by pedestrian postmen serving a given street in London:

> As a general rule, the expenses of a business do not increase by any means proportionally to the quantity of business. Let us take as an example, a set of operations which we are accustomed to see carried on by one great establishment, that of the Post Office. Suppose that the business, let us say only of the London letter-post, instead of being centralized in a single concern, were divided among five or six competing

---

12. *See* Postal Rate and Fee Changes, 1994, Dkt. No. R94-1, at V-10 to V-16 (Postal Rate Commission 1994).
13. MAIL BOXES ETC., 1994 SEC FORM 10-K, at 3 (1994).

companies. Each of these would be obliged to maintain almost as large an establishment as is now sufficient for the whole. Since each must arrange for receiving and delivering letters in all parts of the town, each must send letter-carriers into every street, and almost every alley, and this too as many times in the day as is now done by the Post Office, if the service is to be as well performed. Each must have an office for receiving letters in every neighborhood, with all subsidiary arrangements for collecting the letters from the different offices and re-distributing them. I say nothing of the much greater number of superior officers who would be required to check and control the subordinates, implying not only a greater cost in salaries for such responsible officers, but the necessity, perhaps, of being satisfied in many instances with an inferior standard of qualification, and so failing in the object.[14]

Those economies of scale may have existed 150 years ago in London, but it is far from obvious today that any appreciable economies of scale obtain with the higher mail volumes and population densities in American cities and suburbs.

Certainly the volumetric limits of a mail truck, as well as the weight and volumetric limits of a postman's mail bag, imply *decreasing* returns to scale when the quantity of mail being delivered to a neighborhood reaches a certain level. Even in rural areas, where population density may be low, modern transportation vehicles allow deliveries over a wider area. Even if there are cost savings from a single delivery

---

14. 1 JOHN STUART MILL, PRINCIPLES OF POLITICAL ECONOMY 160-61 (John W. Parker 1848).

provider for rural areas, this need not preclude private provision of such service. Such cost savings are minimal in any case. Even rural areas are served by multiple newspaper delivery routes, which demonstrates that an extremely low-cost service can be maintained simply for the delivery of one item on a daily basis to a substantial proportion of households. In short, nothing inherent in the technology of truck driving and walking justifies government ownership and control of the Postal Service or a monopoly in the delivery of letter mail.

A second alleged economy of scale in door-to-door delivery arises because the cost of making a delivery to a particular location does not depend on the number of pieces delivered there. This relationship means that the Postal Service can lower the average cost of delivering letters to a particular location by increasing the number of pieces delivered. This cost condition does not necessarily imply that only one delivery service should exist, for the rate at which average costs fall depends on the chosen frequency of delivery. A reduction in the frequency of delivery increases the likelihood that multiple pieces will be delivered to a given household and thus reduces the average cost of delivery. Households may differ in their frequency requirements so that not all require daily delivery. Multiple delivery services can provide services of varying quality at lower cost.

Furthermore, to the extent that the Postal Service can achieve economies of scale in delivery, they may reflect a failure of the Postal Rate Commission's current regulation of the quality of postal services.[15] The Postal Service can influence the extent of economies of scale in delivery by the level of quality it sets—such as the number of deliveries per day or week, the average number of days necessary to deliver a letter, and so forth. Economies of scale in delivery (that is,

---

15. *See* J. Gregory Sidak, *The Economics of Mail Delivery: Commentary*, in GOVERNING THE POSTAL SERVICE, *supra* note 9, at 14, 14–15.

Technological Justifications 51

the probability that there will be two or more pieces for delivery to a single mail stop on a given delivery run) increase as delivery becomes less frequent, the mail stream moves more slowly, the volume of non-time-sensitive mail delivered by the Postal Service (such as parcels and second class mail) rises, and non-time-sensitive mail is priced at lower levels that reflect a smaller allocation of common fixed costs. Thus, to the extent that the Postal Service's intellectual defense for the continuation of the statutory monopoly over letter mail is predicated on the existence of scale economies in delivery, the Postal Service can increase the magnitude of those economies—though at a cost to consumers—by attributing as few costs as possible to other classes of mail.

Stated differently, if the frequency of delivery were market driven, the Postal Service's alleged economies of scale would vanish. We do not observe, for example, "natural monopoly" delivery services in each metropolitan or rural area that act as common carriers for delivering pizza, appliances, furniture, or nursery products. Why not? Because any gains from exploiting economies of scale are more than offset by other aspects of service quality that derive from controlling one's own delivery network.[16]

A third potential source of economies of scale in door-to-door delivery is that, increasingly, a postman does not really go all the way to the customer's door. Consumers cannot buy higher-quality mail service from the Postal Service the way they can buy higher-quality services from private suppliers of goods and services. The delivery of mail in new suburban neighborhoods, for example, is typically to a group of boxes that may be seventy-five feet or more from the customer's home. The customer in effect completes the last leg of the delivery. He cannot pay the Postal Service to deliv-

---

16. We thank Robert Crandall for helping us to sharpen this argument and for suggesting the pizza example.

er to his door. This truncation of services offered by the Postal Service directly relates to the question of economies of scale in delivery. Aggregated mailboxes in newer neighborhoods, for example, reduce the cost of delivery for the Postal Service but impose a delivery cost on mail recipients, who must walk from their homes to get their mail. This cost will vary from consumer to consumer and could be considerable for some, such as an older person forced to walk in snowy, rainy, or icy conditions to her mailbox. Thus, the economies of scale that some claim to exist over the delivery function may come at greater private cost to consumers. If so, they are false economies indeed.[17]

Collection of Mail. The Postal Service operates nearly 40,000 post offices, stations, and branches.[18] There is nothing to distinguish an office building used by the Postal Service from any other type of structure in commerce or industry. Consequently, buildings used by the Postal Service do not inherently

---

17. *See* Sidak, *The Economics of Mail Delivery: Commentary, supra* note 15, at 15-16. Judge Douglas Ginsburg, for example, has noted that a consumer

> cannot buy door-to-door service because, under the postal regulation, the mail goes only to the street . . . . [Further], there is only daily service, and increasingly less of it. You cannot sign up for twice-daily service. And you cannot say, "I'll pay less to receive twice-weekly service," because you do not pay on the receiving end. This high degree of uniformity and standardization that has become normal in the Postal Service—even the postal box has to conform to postal regulations—is emblematic of the potential loss in consumer satisfaction, consumer surplus, and consumer welfare that we associate with the old integrated telephone system.

The Economics of Mail Delivery: Discussion, in GOVERNING THE POSTAL SERVICE, *supra* note 9, at 19 (remarks of Douglas H. Ginsburg).

18. U.S. POSTAL SERVICE, 1994 ANNUAL REP. 37 (1995).

Technological Justifications 53

have a natural monopoly property.

Collection of incoming mail from post offices or mail boxes (of which there are 300,000) also is not a natural monopoly, because collection can be accomplished as effectively or at lower cost by other service providers, including retail stores and private post offices such as Mail Boxes Etc. Indeed, these private competitors provide a yardstick for assessing the extent to which the Postal Service has failed to innovate in its retail services. A typical Mail Boxes Etc. center offers mail and parcel receiving, packaging, and parcel shipping services through a number of carriers, and provides small businesses with telephone message service, word processing, copying and printing, office supplies, and communications services such as fax, voice mail, pagers, electronic transmission of income tax returns, and wire transfers of funds. The center also offers stamps, packaging supplies, stationery supplies, keys, passport photos, and film processing.[19] In contrast, not until 1994 did the board of governors approve the use of credit and debit cards to pay for Postal Service products and services, and national implementation of the system for handling such transactions was not scheduled to occur until April 1995.[20] Moreover, unlike all post offices, the mail receiving service of Mail Boxes Etc. is accessible to customers twenty-four hours a day.[21]

As in the case of final delivery of mail to the house-

---

19. MAIL BOXES ETC., 1994 SEC FORM 10-K, at 2 (1994).
20. 1994 COMPREHENSIVE STATEMENT, *supra* note 5, at 3.
21. MAIL BOXES ETC., 1994 SEC FORM 10-K, at 2 (1994). It is a further comment on the degree to which the Postal Service lags behind private firms that, in filings with the Securities and Exchange Commission, Mail Boxes Etc. "does not view the U.S. Postal Service or other foreign postal services as direct competitors." *Id.* at 11. "Although the Company offers similar services, such as private mail receiving service and parcel handling, neither the U.S. Postal Service nor foreign postal services generally offer ancillary business support, communications and personal services offered by [Mail Boxes Etc.] Centers." *Id.*

hold, an accurate assessment of the economic costs of mail collection must include the costs incurred by purchasers of postal services. There is evidence that any economies of scale that may arise from central collection of incoming mail are achieved at a high cost to consumers in terms of travel to the post office and the time-cost of waiting in line. Those costs are entirely real and, when added to those costs of collection that the Postal Service chooses to recognize, strongly imply that greater reliance on scattered small-scale sites would lower the total social costs of mail collection. Thus, private provision of mail collection would improve cost efficiency.

As of 1994, the Postal Service had $16.2 billion invested in property and equipment.[22] There is nothing inherent in government ownership and control over those facilities used to provide local distribution service that would suggest the presence of cost savings from unified ownership and control. Like the buildings, there is nothing to distinguish the equipment from any other type of privately operated capital equipment, such as warehouse sorting equipment used by wholesalers and retail chains. The operation of sorting equipment may exhibit some economies of scale, but there is no apparent reason why such economies would differ from those of any other capital equipment used in manufacturing. Furthermore, it is clear that such economies, if they exist, are highly localized and do not in any way justify the national or regional scope of postal operations. Finally, the equipment is not transaction-specific and is not part of a transmission network such as electric transmission wires, buried telephone cable, natural gas pipelines, or water and sewer pipelines. Thus, the sorting equipment used by the Postal Service cannot be said to exhibit the natural monopoly property.

---

22. 1994 COMPREHENSIVE STATEMENT, *supra* note 5, at 44.

Summary and Implications

None of the components of postal service—contracting for long-distance transportation, regional sortation and transportation, or local collection, sortation, and delivery—exhibits the natural monopoly property. The Postal Service's continued statutory monopoly over letter mail therefore cannot rest on the assertion that it is reaping for American consumers the benefits of a natural monopoly technology. There are, consequently, no cost-efficiency grounds for restricting entry or preventing competition in postal markets.

THE FALLACY THAT THE POSTAL SERVICE MUST BE A NATIONWIDE FULL-SERVICE CARRIER

Economies of scope are used to justify preserving a multiproduct natural monopoly for the Postal Service. Moreover, the possibility of achieving additional economies of scope by expansion into new markets is used to argue for *extension* of the postal monopoly. The Postal Service seeks to increase its presence in parcel post, express mail, and other services because it is asserted that there are increasing returns to producing those services jointly with letter mail. Its reasoning seems to be that any additional contribution to overhead, no matter how small, justifies a new line of business.

A firm's technology is said to exhibit economies of scope if a single firm can produce two products at a lower cost than if each product were produced by a different firm.[23] The cost of producing one of the products alone is referred to as its *stand-alone cost*.[24] Economies of scope are said to exist

---

23. An early exposition of economies of scope is John C. Panzar & Robert D. Willig, *Economies of Scale in Multi-Output Production*, 91 Q.J. ECON. 481 (1977). For subsequent discussions, see SPULBER, *supra* note 1, at 114–17.

24. *See, e.g.,* BAUMOL & SIDAK, *supra* note 11, at 58–59.

if the sum of the stand-alone costs of the two products exceeds the cost of joint production. In the multiproduct case, a production technology is said to have the natural monopoly property if a single firm can provide the bundle of products (such as cars and trucks, or the delivery of letters and parcels) at a lower cost than can two or more firms.

Economies of scope often stem from sharing joint and common costs across a range of services. That sharing might take the form of common overhead costs for the production of multiple products or services. The use of hub-and-spoke systems in network industries creates economies of scope if the usage density is higher on each branch in comparison with a point-to-point system. The sharing of trunk lines to connect multiple branches in a network creates economies of scope in comparison with stand-alone systems that duplicate the trunk-line facility.

An assessment of economies of scope depends on how the firm's products or services are defined. Products can be delineated arbitrarily on the basis of product features, customer characteristics, location, time available, brand names, and so on. Postal services such as first, second, third, and fourth class, parcel post, and express mail represent arbitrary historical classifications based largely on the content of the mail. Those services can share overhead depending on how the postal delivery service is organized.

Yet, for the same reasons that it is implausible that the production technology for postal delivery exhibits the natural monopoly property, it is also implausible that there are substantial economies of scope in postal delivery. Because transportation is contracted out to independent carriers, the Postal Service cannot be said to realize any economies of scope at this stage; the fact that multiple independent providers actually perform the transportation services negates any economies of scope resulting from a single service provider. Regional sortation and delivery can exhibit economies of scope only to the extent that two types of mail are routed through the same facilities. Local delivery can exhibit some economies of scope again to the extent that, say, first and third class mail are sorted and delivered together, but not if the services are provided independently.

In any case, the presence of economies of scope is not sufficient to justify the postal monopoly. Multiple carriers can each achieve economies of scope if each offers multiple services. United Parcel Service, for example, offers delivery for both overnight mail and parcels.

Moreover, economies of scope do not justify extending the postal monopoly. On the contrary, the presence of economies of scope would more plausibly imply the need to *eliminate* the postal monopoly. There are currently private carriers of express mail—such as Federal Express and United Parcel Service, to name only two—that are not permitted to carry standard letter mail. If there are economies of scope between standard letter mail and express mail service, those private carriers could realize those economies if the Private Express Statutes did not exist. Thus, potential economies of scope do not imply any need to extend the government's postal monopoly. Rather, they imply the need to extend the range of permissible privately supplied services.

A private firm considering entry into a market will determine whether its stand-alone cost for a given product would be less than the prevailing price for that product in that market.[25] Of course, the prospective entrant is free to enter by simultaneously offering two or more products over which it can achieve economies of scope. For example, because an alternative advertising carrier already provides service to a neighborhood, the carrier's cost of entering the business of delivering first class letters no longer would be the stand-alone cost of letter delivery; rather, the cost of entry would be the incremental cost of adding letter delivery given that the carrier

---

25. *See, e.g.,* BAUMOL & SIDAK, *supra* note 11, at 77-78.

already delivers unaddressed advertising. Stated differently, the cost to the alternative advertising carrier of entering the letter delivery business would be the stand-alone cost of first class letter delivery minus the economies of scope (on a unit basis) derivable from the firm's joint delivery of unaddressed advertising and first class letter mail.

The same analysis of the incremental cost of entry would apply to the multiproduct activities of the Postal Service were it not for the fact that the firm is a publicly owned and controlled enterprise. The Postal Service delivers mail categorized by five general classes. If competition exists for four of those classes, it is unnecessary for the Postal Service to offer the fifth in conjunction with one or more of the other four classes *even if* the Postal Service could achieve economies of scope by providing them jointly with the one noncompetitive class of mail. To conclude otherwise is to succumb to the fallacy that the Postal Service must be a nationwide full-service carrier of all varieties of mail. To the contrary, the proper scope of market entry by a government-owned firm should be defined by the scope of the market failure that this form of government intervention seeks to redress, not by the cost-minimizing scope of a public firm that produces both competitive and noncompetitive products. Indeed, if significant economies of scope exist between competitive and noncompetitive products, then the more natural question to ask is why the superior regime is not private provision of *all* the products, subject perhaps to the usual price regulation, safeguards, cost allocation, nondiscrimination requirements in the sale of access to bottleneck facilities, and so forth.

The GAO assumes that the Postal Service must be "a nationwide full-service provider of postal services."[26] That assumption, however, has no basis in economic theory. If

---

26. GENERAL ACCOUNTING OFFICE, U.S. POSTAL PRICING: PRICING POSTAL SERVICES IN A COMPETITIVE ENVIRONMENT 8 (1992).

competition is feasible in a particular class of mail, as the evidence in parcel post and overnight mail amply demonstrates, then there is no market failure necessitating government involvement in the first place. There is *a fortiori* no need for the government itself to provide such service and thereby compete against private firms.

The same reasoning applies to the geographic scope of coverage for a particular service that private firms are capable of providing: There is no need for the Postal Service to provide that service in locales where private firms can profitably provide it. It is doubtful, for example, that *any* postal service in Manhattan must be provided by a public enterprise. As a practical matter, of course, the geographic scope of private services is not an issue of controversy, because firms like United Parcel Service and Federal Express provide service throughout the United States.

In his call for the Postal Service to be "a nationwide full-service provider of postal services,"[27] Postmaster General Runyon seemed to be implicitly asking the following question: What is the minimum efficient scope of the firm? This is a subtle question that has intrigued economists for decades. The problem, however, is that the correct answer to the question depends on whether one is addressing a private firm (such as Federal Express) or a publicly owned and controlled firm (such as the Postal Service) whose mission is to correct some demonstrable market failure.

In short, economic analysis offers no rationale why the Postal Service should have to provide consumers every type of mail service or provide any particular type of service to consumers in all regions of the country. Sound public policy dictates that scarce government resources should be confined to producing *only* those postal services which some form of

---

27. Address by Postmaster General Marvin Runyon to the National Press Club, Washington, D.C. (Jan. 31, 1995) (available in LEXIS News Library).

market failure prevents private firms from profitably providing to consumers. The practical implication of this principle is that the Postal Service should aspire to do *less* by exiting any market that is demonstrably competitive.

Conclusion

The Postal Service is not a natural monopoly. In contracting for long-distance transportation, in regional sortation and transportation, and in local collection, sortation, and delivery, the assertion that the Postal Service is a natural monopoly is implausible as a matter of economic analysis. If anything, economic analysis suggests that the Postal Service has considerable incentive and latitude to truncate consumer choices so as to increase the false appearance that economies of scale and scope exist in local delivery. We can identify no intellectually defensible argument that the Postal Service's statutory monopoly under the Private Express Statutes flows directly from a natural monopoly that it purports to possess over mail delivery.

To the contrary, if economies of scope exist between letter mail and other classes of mail, that fact would strongly support *repeal* of the Private Express Statutes rather than expansion of the Postal Service into competitive lines of business. Sound public policy should encourage the entry of private firms into mail services currently monopolized by the federal government rather than extend the government's monopoly into markets that private firms have already proven to be demonstrably competitive.

4

Public Provision of Postal Services

IS IT NECESSARY for the government to provide the full range of postal services that consumers demand? No, we argue in this chapter. In the United States public provision of postal services differs significantly from the regulated private ownership and control that typify telecommunications, natural gas, electricity, and cable television, and that formerly typified the now-deregulated airline, trucking, bus, and railroad industries. Continued public provision of postal services is also contrary to the movement toward privatization in numerous industries in the United States and abroad.[1] Our analysis

---

1. *See* George L. Priest, *Socialism, Eastern Europe, and the Question of the Postal Monopoly, in* GOVERNING THE POSTAL SERVICE 46 (J. Gregory Sidak ed., AEI Press 1994). For a discussion of the extensive privatization initiatives in the United Kingdom, see JOHN VICKERS & GEORGE YARROW, PRIVATIZATION: AN ECONOMIC ANALYSIS (MIT Press 1988). For a discussion of privatization of postal services, see Michael A. Crew & Paul R. Kleindorfer, *Pricing, Entry, Service Quality, and Innovation under a Commercialized Postal Service, in* GOVERNING THE POSTAL SERVICE, *supra*, at 150, 151–57.

will show that public provision of postal services in the United States cannot be justified by any possible market failure. It is apparent that competitive private firms effectively provide a wide variety of communication, delivery, and transportation services. The elimination of government restrictions on entry into postal services would lead to a significant increase in privately provided services.

The two principal reasons given today for public provision of postal services are the social goal of providing universal service, and the need to ensure the security of the mail stream. Earlier in American history, the justifications for public provision of postal services included the dissemination of military intelligence, censorship, and the promotion of commerce, personal correspondence, national unity, and the diffusion of knowledge.[2] The only two means of communication were face-to-face conversation or transportation of written words. We do not discuss those historical justifications because technological change and market developments provide many alternative means of communication that have long since eliminated the need to rely on the Postal Service to achieve those objectives. Indeed, the elimination of those outdated justifications reveals how intellectually flimsy is the case for continued public provision of postal services.

We show in this chapter that the two contemporary justifications for public provision of postal services are inconsistent with current technological and market developments in communications, delivery, and transportation services in the United States. There is, consequently, no reason to continue public provision of postal services. Postal delivery has no insurmountable technological barriers to entry, and indeed extensive competitive provision of postal services already

---

2. *See* WAYNE E. FULLER, THE AMERICAN MAIL: ENLARGER OF THE COMMON LIFE 79–147 (University of Chicago Press 1972); William Ty Mayton, *The Mission and Methods of the Postal Service, in* GOVERNING THE POSTAL SERVICE, *supra* note 1, at 60, 79–83.

takes place. Further, postal services need not be publicly provided either to ensure ubiquity of service and pricing uniformity, or to ensure the integrity of the mail stream.

THE ABSENCE OF INSURMOUNTABLE TECHNOLOGICAL BARRIERS TO ENTRY IN POSTAL DELIVERY

There do not appear to be any insurmountable technological barriers to entry in postal delivery. An economic entry barrier is a cost that must be borne by an entrant but not by an incumbent.[3] The main barrier to entry that raises concerns in a regulated market is the problem of sunk costs. An incumbent firm can write off its irreversible costs of capital and thus only need be concerned about its variable costs in setting its prices. In contrast, an entrant not only must recover variable costs, but also must earn revenues that cover its irreversible entry costs. Sunk costs are a concern in network industries such as electricity and natural gas because the costs of transmission facilities are irreversible and transaction-specific.[4]

The postal system is often referred to as a network industry because any transportation and delivery system has many of the features of a network, particularly in terms of dispersed collection and delivery and centralized sorting. This

---

3. DANIEL F. SPULBER, REGULATION AND MARKETS 40-41 (MIT Press 1989); GEORGE J. STIGLER, THE ORGANIZATION OF INDUSTRY 67 (Richard D. Irwin, Inc. 1968); William J. Baumol & Robert D. Willig, *Fixed Cost, Sunk Cost, Entry Barriers and Sustainability of Monopoly*, 95 Q.J. ECON. 405, 418 (1981).

4. As Paul Milgrom and John Roberts note, "the *specificity* of an asset is measured as the percentage of investment value that is lost when the asset is used outside the specific setting or relationship." PAUL MILGROM & JOHN ROBERTS, ECONOMICS, ORGANIZATION AND MANAGEMENT 135 (Prentice Hall 1992) (emphasis in original). Both fixed and variable costs may have components that are transaction-specific and thus nonsalvageable. *See* OLIVER E. WILLIAMSON, THE ECONOMIC INSTITUTIONS OF CAPITALISM 52-56 (Free Press 1985).

analogy does not, however, imply that the capital equipment of a postal delivery system is in any way comparable to that of a transmission network composed of pipelines or electric lines. To the contrary, equipment for the postal system is far from being an irreversible investment and is certainly not transaction-specific.

The capital of the Postal Service consists of buildings, vehicles, and sorting equipment. The buildings, which may be leased rather than owned, can be put to other uses and are not tied to any particular customer location. Vehicles are obviously mobile assets. Although it is true that mail trucks have a specialized design unique to the Postal Service, the same is true of the distinctive trucks of United Parcel Service, which are manufactured by various suppliers according to the company's specifications. The services of sorting equipment, while specialized, are not tied to a particular customer, for they can be transferred across markets simply by transporting the items to be sorted to and from different locations. For example, Federal Express sorts packages for domestic destinations at its "SuperHub" in Memphis, at a second national hub in Indianapolis (where the Postal Service also has built its Eagle Hub), at regional hubs in Newark and Oakland, and at metropolitan sorting facilities in Los Angeles and Chicago.[5]

Most of the Postal Service's investment of $16.2 billion in buildings, equipment, and land is not sunk, for it can be easily recovered in the marketplace. The nonsalvageable portion of that investment is minuscule when compared with the Postal Service's annual revenues of roughly $50 billion. Moreover, assets such as sorting equipment and vehicles have relatively short economic lives—unlike transmission facilities in such network industries as natural gas, electric power, and long-distance telecommunications—and thus do not represent an insurmountable entry barrier. Therefore, sunk costs are not

---

5. FEDERAL EXPRESS CORP., 1994 SEC FORM 10-K, at 4 (1994).

large in this industry, and the incumbency of the Postal Service does not confer on it a decided advantage over potential entrants.

Finally, competitive entry into delivery services *already has occurred*. Indeed, for parcels, private entry by United Parcel Service began *before* the Post Office started offering parcel post on January 1, 1913.[6] Actual competitive entry demonstrates conclusively that entry barriers are not an issue.

Many package delivery services have made substantial investments in delivery. Companies in package delivery include Air Express International, Airborne Freight, American Freightways, Consolidated Freightways, DHL Worldwide Express, Greyhound Lines, Inc., Roadway Services, Inc., and United Parcel Service; express carriers include Federal Express, United Parcel Service, Airborne Freight, and Em-

---

6. GERALD CULLINAN, THE POST OFFICE DEPARTMENT 106 (Frederick A. Praeger 1968). By 1916, the Post Office was offering parcel post services at rates less than half of freight rates charged by private firms. *Id.* at 196. When residents of Vernal, Utah, discovered those low rates, they began mailing bricks by parcel post from Salt Lake City, 150 miles away, to construct a new bank building. "The influx of brick parcels strained the facilities of the Vernal post office and reduced the local letter carriers to a state of exhaustion, but the bank still stands—two stories high, covering most of a city block." *Id.* It would appear that the Post Office's price was below both short-run and long-run measures of incremental cost, for it abruptly discontinued such services despite a surge in demand:

> While Vernal was building its bank, farmers in Utah caught the idea and started sending their produce to market by parcel post. In desperation, the Post Office Department, without even consulting Congress, hurriedly issued a regulation putting a limit of 200 pounds on the weight of parcel post that one individual could send another in a single day.

Id. at 196–97.

ery/Purolator.[7] The rapid rate of growth and economic success of those firms show that the cost of investment is not preventing competitive entry in postal delivery. The same holds for the growth and planned expansion of second and third class mail delivery companies, such as Alternate Postal Delivery, Inc. (formerly United Delivery Systems, Inc.),[8] and Time Warner's Publishers Express, Inc.[9] The technology of those delivery services can be adapted to other types of mail, including letter mail. In short, it is abundantly clear that private firms are capable of providing postal services.

COST ECONOMIES DO NOT JUSTIFY PUBLIC PROVISION OF POSTAL SERVICES

Although the postal delivery service is clearly not a natural monopoly for the reasons explained in chapter 3, any cost economies, if they did exist, would not justify public provision of the full range of postal services by the Postal Service. First, public ownership of an enterprise inherently impedes maximizing economic welfare because the incentives for productive efficiency and cost minimization are absent. Second, private ownership of the facilities does not in any way impair the efficient operation of those facilities.

The *possibility* that technological cost economies may be present does not guarantee that they will be achieved. In

---

7. *See, e.g.*, AIRBORNE FREIGHT CORP., 1994 SEC FORM 10-K, at 3 (1995); AMERICAN FREIGHTWAYS CORP., 1994 SEC FORM 10-K, at 3 (1995); CONSOLIDATED FREIGHTWAYS, INC., 1994 SEC FORM 10-K, at 3–5 (1995); CORPORATE PROFILE FOR DHL WORLDWIDE EXPRESS, BUS. WIRE, INC. (Sept. 9, 1994); FEDERAL EXPRESS CORP., 1994 SEC FORM 10-K, at 1 (1994); GREYHOUND LINES, INC., 1994 SEC FORM 10-K, at 3 (1995); ROADWAY SERVICES, INC., 1994 SEC FORM 10-K, at 1–5 (1995).

8. ALTERNATE POSTAL DELIVERY, INC., REGISTRATION STATEMENT FOR INITIAL PUBLIC OFFERING OF 1,000,000 SHARES OF COMMON STOCK (Aug. 2, 1995).

9. TIME WARNER INC., 1994 SEC FORM 10-K, at I-8 (1995).

his landmark study of economies of scale and scope, the business historian Alfred D. Chandler observes that managerial skill is required to attain those economies that are technologically available.[10] Private owners have an incentive to maximize profits because they are the residual claimants to the returns on their investment. This state of affairs gives private owners an incentive to engage in oversight of managerial performance to guarantee that productive efficiency is achieved and that costs are minimized. Owners will provide managers with incentives for cost minimization.

Public ownership eliminates or severely reduces monitoring and oversight incentives. As a consequence, public ownership and control reduce incentives for cost minimization. The Postal Service is not a profit-maximizing enterprise and does not pay dividends on its invested capital.[11] Nor is the Postal Service subject to effective revenue constraints, for it has a protected monopoly in letter mail and can raise rates to recover costs.

The Postal Service's difficulties in carrying out automation illustrate its failure to achieve technical efficiencies. The Postal Service discontinued central management over automation after the 1992 reorganization, which subsequently led to problems in implementing the new technology.[12] As a consequence, field managers complained about the lack of central direction, and the Postal Service reestablished a central office to oversee automation.[13] In February 1995 the GAO

---

10. ALFRED D. CHANDLER, SCALE AND SCOPE: THE DYNAMICS OF INDUSTRIAL CAPITALISM 17 (Harvard University Press 1990); *see also* Daniel F. Spulber, *Economic Analysis and Management Strategy: A Survey Continued*, 3 J. ECON. & MGMT. STRATEGY 355, 378 (1994).

11. See Henry B. Hansmann, *The Postal Service as a Public Enterprise: Commentary, in* GOVERNING THE POSTAL SERVICE, *supra* note 1, at 39, 42–43 (discussing capital allocation for the Postal Service).

12. GENERAL ACCOUNTING OFFICE, POSTAL SERVICE: AUTOMATION IS TAKING LONGER AND PRODUCING LESS THAN EXPECTED 2 (1995).

13. *Id.*

concluded: "The savings from automation continue to be small compared to overall labor costs and more difficult to achieve than the Service anticipated."[14] Similarly, Paul MacAvoy and George McIsaac found that the Postal Service's automation program, the largest capitalization plan in any public sector service organization in the 1980s and 1990s, caused the Postal Service to have significantly higher capital costs but not significantly lower labor costs.[15]

Automation of Postal Service letter mail processing began in 1982.[16] The Postal Service acquired optical character readers that could recognize zip codes and print bar codes on letters, and specialized equipment to sort mail automatically by reading bar codes. The Postal Service reorganized its workforce to take advantage of investment in automation equipment. In addition, it offered incentives to mailers to print their own bar codes. When it is completed in 1997, the automation program will represent 14,000 pieces of equipment at a cost of over $5 billion.[17]

How has the automation program fared? From 1982 through 1987, the Postal Service deployed 1,129 optical character readers, and by 1992 it installed 1,369 bar code scanners. Additional equipment permits delivery sorting and bar coding of mail from a remote location. In 1983 the addition of four digits to the zip code permitted sorting to specific segments of the carrier's route. According to the GAO, bar coding is falling substantially behind the Postal Service's schedule. To correct the difficulties that optical character readers are having in deriving bar codes from addresses, the

---

14. *Id.*

15. Paul W. MacAvoy & George S. McIsaac, *The Current File on the Case for Privatization of the Federal Government Enterprises*, 4 HUME PAPERS ON PUB. POL'Y (forthcoming 1995).

16. The following discussion on the Postal Service automation program relies on the GAO's 1995 report, *supra* note 12.

17. *Id.* at 2.

Postal Service is making further investments in computer and camera enhancements.[18]

There appears to be a fundamental inconsistency between incentives given to mailers for bar coding and those for presorting. Rate reductions for bar coding shift the sorting function to the Postal Service and the coding function to the mailer. In response to those incentives, private mailers have met and exceeded Postal Service coding targets. In contrast, rate incentives for presorting by mailers shift the sorting function to the mailer, but require additional sorting by the Postal Service or letter carrier to be merged with bar-coded mail. The Postal Service has not made a clear choice between the sorting and coding function, and this vacillation is reflected in the conflicting signals to mailers. On balance, bar coding by mailers is being discouraged, and the Postal Service is increasing its investment expenditures and personnel levels to bar code the mail itself.[19]

Investment in automation has not yielded projected savings in labor costs. The GAO notes that Postal Service predictions of labor savings, which accounted for letter volume growth, have fallen short. The GAO states: "Work-years in manual letter sorting, which should decline as the Service turns to automation, actually increased 5.3 percent in 1993 and 2.9 percent in 1994."[20] Moreover, the expected shift to temporary employees as the result of automation has not been realized, as career employment has returned to the levels that existed before reorganization.[21] The Postal Service's automation difficulties do not suggest any inherent advantage to public provision of mail sortation and delivery.

Private ownership of the facilities used to deliver the mail certainly would not prevent a company from achieving

---

18. *Id.* at 21.
19. *Id.* at 29–33.
20. *Id.* at 43.
21. *Id.* at 44.

cost economies. Economic analysis demonstrates that competition serves to stimulate owners and managers to minimize costs. This incentive means that competitive firms would realize the technologically available economies of scale. Moreover, economic analysis shows that the existence of economies of scale is consistent with a market's being populated by competitive firms, for the pressure of potential competition from new entrants provides pricing and cost discipline to incumbent firms. Thus, the natural monopoly argument is not a sufficient condition for barring entry into the market for letter mail because competitive, privately owned companies can realize the benefits of any increasing returns to scale that might obtain.

PUBLIC PROVISION IS NOT NEEDED TO ENSURE UBIQUITY AND PRICING UNIFORMITY

Perhaps the most popular argument for public ownership and control of the Postal Service is to ensure service of the same quality for the same price delivered anywhere in the country, as required by the Postal Reorganization Act of 1970.[22] The shorthand for this objective is "universal service," but that label fails to convey that the service to be provided must be priced *uniformly* throughout the country. The Postal Service's 1994 *Comprehensive Statement on Postal Operations* states:

> To protect the revenue base of the postal system, the Private Express Statutes have long restricted the private carriage of letters for compensation. The statutes go hand-in-hand with a singular obligation to provide a universal mail service at uniform rates throughout the nation. But the statutes will not be sufficient,

---

22. 39 U.S.C. § 3623(d).

alone, to preserve a system of universal mail service with uniform rates:

The Postal Service must become a more assertive, responsive, and effective competitor, keeping its customers and attracting new ones through the value and satisfaction that its services, in totality, provide.

A successfully competitive, but partially protected postal system is not achievable without special challenges. Effective enforcement of the statutes presupposes that the American people and their institutions will continue to value and respect the concepts of universal mail service and uniform rates, neither of which would be likely to survive without the statutes. The Postal Service bears a responsibility to serve its customers well enough overall that they will continue to demand the type of universal mail system it provides.[23]

Thus, the Postal Service views universal service as the justification not only for retaining its existing monopoly over letter mail, but also for expanding its operations in and into competitive markets.

Moreover, the Postal Service publicly romanticizes its universal service function in a manner that surely is disproportionate to the magnitude of that undertaking. In May 1995, for example, the Postal Service took out a quarter-page advertisement on the op-ed page of the *New York Times* to tout its deliveries by bush pilot above the Arctic Circle and by

---

23. U.S. POSTAL SERVICE, COMPREHENSIVE STATEMENT ON POSTAL OPERATIONS, FY 1994, at 36 (1995) [hereinafter 1994 COMPREHENSIVE STATEMENT].

mailboat in the Louisiana bayous.[24] Those deliveries to remote, high-cost areas also include Supai, Arizona, where, the Postal Service explains, pack mules must negotiate eight miles of trails down the south rim of the Grand Canyon to deliver not only mail, but also food and furniture to the Havasupai Indian Reservation below.[25] One wonders how the Havasupai managed to procure food and furniture before the U.S. mail came along. One can ask similar questions about groceries and tires delivered by mail to the Alaskan wilderness.[26]

Uniform pricing may have an efficiency justification in the sense that it reduces the transactions costs of sending mail. Of course, it also has a powerful distributional effect, as the Supai mule trail illustrates. Given the differences in the cost of delivery between urban and rural areas, the requirement of uniform pricing necessarily implies that some customers will subsidize other customers. Is public control of postal services the *only* means to achieve ubiquity of service, uniformity of pricing, and subsidies to high-cost delivery areas? The answer is plainly no. Is public control the *most efficient* means of achieving those social policies? Again, no.

First, private firms like Federal Express and United Parcel Service provide ubiquitous service at a uniform price, which in turn implies a subsidization of high-cost recipients of overnight mail and parcels. The accomplishment of those goals of the Postal Reorganization Act therefore does not require either public ownership or control of postal services. The breakup of the Bell System and the deregulation of the

---

24. N.Y. TIMES, May 12, 1995, at A31 (Postal Service advertisement). The weekday price of a quarter-page advertisement running one time on the op-ed page of the *New York Times* is $18,315. Telephone interview between Marshall Smith, American Enterprise Institute, and Janine Lloyd, *New York Times* Advertising Dep't, May 23, 1995.

25. U.S. POSTAL SERVICE, HISTORY OF THE UNITED STATES POSTAL SERVICE, 1775–1993, at 20 (1993) (describing Supai mule mail route).

26. *See The Economics of Mail Delivery: Discussion, in* GOVERNING THE POSTAL SERVICE, *supra* note 1, at 21–22.

airlines did not end service to rural areas.[27]

Second, private firms have already shown that they are better able than the Postal Service to provide service at low cost. According to the GAO, the private providers in parcel post and overnight mail "dominate the business-to-business segment because they offer lower priced and higher quality service."[28] The same should hold true of postal services that, by virtue of political judgment, must be priced below cost. Indeed, the Postal Service *already* contracts out delivery to private carriers in some high-cost areas, such as rural areas. The continued reliance on the Postal Service's monopoly over letter mail, however, forecloses experimentation with alternative mechanisms for the private provision of postal service to high-cost areas. In particular, it would be possible in the absence of the statutory monopoly for the federal government to invite bids from private firms to provide mail service to a particular remote area and to assume the obligation of being the carrier of last resort. Postal customers in that region would continue to pay a nationally uniform price for mail, and private firms would submit competing bids to provide such service for the lowest subsidy to be paid by the federal government. The process would not fundamentally differ from that by which the baker submitting the lowest bid is awarded the contract to supply bread to an Army base. An alternative method of providing universal service would be to give subsidies directly to postal customers and then allow the Postal Service (or any other carrier) to charge customer prices reflecting the true cost of service. We describe those alternatives further in chapter 7.

---

27. PAUL W. MACAVOY, INDUSTRY REGULATION AND THE PERFORMANCE OF THE AMERICAN ECONOMY 68, 71 (W.W. Norton & Co. 1992); ROBERT W. CRANDALL, AFTER THE BREAKUP: TELECOMMUNICATIONS IN A MORE COMPETITIVE ERA 106-45 (Brookings Institution 1991).

28. GENERAL ACCOUNTING OFFICE, U.S. POSTAL PRICING: PRICING POSTAL SERVICES IN A COMPETITIVE ENVIRONMENT 3 (1992).

In short, the pursuit of social goals does not require the Postal Service to have a statutory monopoly or to distort postal pricing. The federal government can instead provide subsidies through either of the contracting mechanisms just described. Universal service at a uniform price does not require public control of postal services. Of course, to say that alternative financing schemes for universal service exist is not to say that it would be politically easy to adopt them in lieu of the current scheme of cross-subsidies. The schemes developed by federal and state governments to provide "universality" across infrastructure industries, including public utilities, have repeatedly involved the cross-subsidy's being collected internally by the franchised monopoly firm providing commercial service of the same kind. Integrating universal and commercial services in an internal tax system of the monopoly provider helps to conceal the magnitude and recipients of the cross-subsidy. If those facts were made explicit, the cross-subsidy might prove to be politically embarrassing and cause voters to demand that Congress end or reduce it.

Public Provision Is Not Needed to Ensure the Integrity of the Mail Stream

The need to maintain the security of the mail stream is another justification given for public ownership of the Postal Service. Just as it places prominent advertisements that romanticize its provision of universal service, so also does the Postal Service extravagantly advertise the security of its mail stream. In September 1995, for example, the Postal Service aired a radio advertisement in the Washington, D.C., area in which actor George C. Scott related that, when the owners of the Hope Diamond wanted to move the gem, they sent it by U.S. mail. The advertisement explained that the U.S. mail can be trusted because, for the price of a 32-cent stamp, the customer also receives the benefits of the Postal Inspection Service. It is unlikely, however, that the Postal Service is better able than private firms to provide secure communications and shipments. Indeed, the Postal Service's own record of reliability and security is problematic.

Private Provision of Secure Communications and Deliveries

Public control of postal services is not needed to ensure security for at least four reasons. First, the private sector offers consumers reliable alternatives to the mail for secure communications. Private firms offer reliable alternatives to parcel post and express mail, and they could easily extend those services to letter mail. Moreover, the reliability argument is obsolete because it neglects the many reliable alternatives to communication by mail: newspapers, radio, television, telecommunications, and electronic communication, such as e-mail and facsimile. Even the Postal Service is investigating entering the field of electronic commerce to offer "certification, authentication, encryption, 'electronic postmarks,' and other value-added services," which, the Postal Service asserts, "would be based on [its] established role as a trusted third party to maintain security and protect individual privacy."[29]

Second, the private sector offers consumers an array of security options for their communications and shipments. The market offers many types of security arrangements ranging from specialized couriers to armored cars. Parcel delivery companies have developed bar-coded tracking systems that ensure security and accuracy in locating packages. Those innovations and varied product offerings of private firms respond to the fact that the security needs of individual mailers vary. In contrast, public control of the postal system has provided a uniform level of security that is not tailored to individual needs.

---

29. U.S. POSTAL SERV., 1994 ANNUAL REP. 10 (1994).

Third, there is no economic necessity for the sale of delivery services to be bundled with the implicit sale of insurance for loss of shipment. Indeed, service provided by the Postal Service is uninsured unless the customer specifically buys insurance. In contrast, private carriers may find that in a competitive market consumers do value some degree of bundled insurance for loss of shipments. Federal Express and United Parcel Service provide insurance on every shipment up to $100, with more insurance available at additional cost.

Fourth, the Postal Service contracts out transportation of mail to private airlines, railroads, and trucking firms.[30] That fact indicates that the federal government does not consider itself the only party trustworthy enough to handle the mail.

Reputational Effects of Criminal Wrongdoing or Negligence by Postal Employees

Empirical studies have established that Postal Service workers earn a wage premium of approximately 20 percent over the earnings of workers performing comparable tasks in the private sector.[31] If the Postal Service were unique in its ability to ensure the integrity of the mail stream, that wage premium could be regarded as a bonding mechanism—a quasi rent that postal employees would lose if discharged from their jobs for compromising the integrity of the mail stream.[32] Anecdotal evidence leads one to reject that hypothesis, however, for in

---

30. 1994 COMPREHENSIVE STATEMENT, *supra* note 23, at 13.

31. Jeffrey M. Perloff & Michael L. Wachter, *A Comparative Analysis of Wage Premiums and Industrial Relations in the British Post Office and the United States Postal Service*, in COMPETITION AND INNOVATION IN POSTAL SERVICES 115 (Michael A. Crew & Paul R. Kleindorfer eds., Kluwer Academic Publishers 1991); DOUGLAS K. ADIE, AN EVALUATION OF POSTAL SERVICE WAGE RATES 74 (AEI Press 1977).

32. *See* Benjamin Klein & Keith B. Leffler, *The Role of Market Forces in Assuring Contractual Performance*, 89 J. POL. ECON. 615 (1981).

recent years the Postal Service has damaged its own reputation for honesty and reliability. During 1994, newspapers and magazines carried numerous stories, some of them simply bizarre, of postal workers' destroying or misappropriating mail.

In the Chicago area, caches of undelivered mail were found either abandoned or burning. During the first three and a half months of 1994, postal inspectors found nearly 70,000 pieces of undelivered mail in Chicago, including 5,000 pieces of undelivered first class mail stashed behind the home of a dismissed postman or in the trunk of another postman's car.[33] One postman was arrested and charged with delaying the delivery of the mail, a felony carrying a maximum penalty of five years in prison.[34] A month later, firefighters battling a blaze found sacks of mail bearing Chicago addresses in a postman's condominium.[35] Those incidents prompted *The New Yorker* to publish a lengthy story in October 1994 detailing the frustrations of one postal manager in Chicago who had tried in vain to improve productivity.[36] The postmaster general subsequently dismissed the mail-burning incident in Chicago as an unfortunate aberration that had attracted excessive attention:

> I think that there's a lot of reporting on the Postal Service on one-of-a-kind type things that happen that [get] nationwide coverage. You know, for example, in Chicago we had . . . things happen—really bad things; they shouldn't

---

33. *More Undelivered Mail Found in Chicago*, N.Y. TIMES, Apr. 16, 1994, § 1, at 6.
34. *Id.*; *see* 18 U.S.C. § 1703 (delay or destruction of mail or newspapers).
35. *Firemen Find Sacks of Mail*, N.Y. TIMES, May 10, 1994, § A, at 12.
36. Jonathan Franzen, *Lost in the Mail*, THE NEW YORKER, Oct. 24, 1994, at 62.

> have happened, but they did. We had a carrier who was a casual employee for three months [and] hadn't delivered the mail. Threw it over a viaduct and a homeless person burned it. That was bad.[37]

To the contrary, the incidents in Chicago were not isolated events, for similar destruction or misappropriation of mail was occurring in Washington, D.C.

In July 1994 the Postal Service disclosed that a Price Waterhouse study revealed that Washington, D.C., had the worst mail service in the nation during the quarter ending May 27, 1994, with only 60.6 percent of first class mail arriving on time.[38] A week later, a surprise audit of three postal facilities in greater Washington, D.C., by the U.S. Postal Inspection Service uncovered more than three million pieces of undelivered mail, some of it dating to February 1994 and mostly stashed in parked trailers.[39] The trade press reported that "[p]ostal inspectors noted in their report that postal workers were reluctant to report delays in handling mail because it could possibly ruin their careers, subjecting them to harsh criticism by supervisors."[40]

---

37. Address by Postmaster General Marvin Runyon to the National Press Club, Washington, D.C. (Jan. 31, 1995) (available in LEXIS News Library).

38. Bill Miller, *Post Offices Playing Catch-up; Workers on Overtime to Speed up Delivery*, WASH. POST, July 24, 1994, at B1; Bill McAllister, *Post Office Acts to End Backlog; Overtime Is Ordered for Area Mail Clerks Today and Sunday*, WASH. POST, July 23, 1994, at A1; Bill McAllister, *Millions of Letters Undelivered; Local Facilities Held Unprocessed Mail*, WASH. POST, July 20, 1994, at A1.

39. Paul M. Alberta, *Probers Find Mail Stashed in Trailers*, DM NEWS, July 25, 1994, at 3. The stashed mail included 2.3 million pieces of bulk business mail and 800,000 first class letters in parked Postal Service trailers at Capitol Heights, Maryland; more than 900,000 pieces of unprocessed mail at Merrifield, Virginia; and thousands of first class letters at Washington's main post office. *Id.*

40. *Id.*

In October 1994 the Postal Service suffered even greater embarrassment when postal inspectors arrested a Washington, D.C., postman for stockpiling four truckloads of undelivered mail in his apartment; workers had to don surgical masks and robes to remove the mail, for the efficiency apartment was overrun by a dog, fifteen birds, and forty-three turtles, and the mail had become saturated by excrement and the putrescent carcasses of more birds and turtles.[41] Even when confiscated, the mail could not be delivered: "Health officials, who . . . seal[ed] the undelivered mail in plastic bags, said they fear the letters may be contaminated by bacteria from the animal carcasses found crammed in the efficiency apartment . . . ."[42] The postmaster general subsequently confirmed, in response to a written question posed by a member of the House Subcommittee on the Postal Service, that less than 1 percent of the 22,800 pieces of stolen mail was "deliverable or salvageable."[43]

Although the cumulative effect of such press reports on the reputation of the Postal Service is difficult to quantify, clearly they can only reduce consumer confidence in this public enterprise. By comparison, a private firm whose reputation is sullied by revelations of negligence or intentional misconduct suffers a statistically significant loss in its stock price.[44] Moreover, the loss exceeds the amount of expected

---

41. Ruben Castaneda & Linda Wheeler, *Dead, Ailing Animals Found in D.C. Postal Worker's Home; Allegedly Stolen Mail Also in NW Apartment*, WASH. POST, Oct. 19, 1994, at B1; Linda Wheeler, *New Homes Found for Animals in Postal Worker's Menagerie*, WASH. POST, Dec. 5, 1994, at D5.

42. Scott Bowles & Toni Locy, *Discovered Mail May Be Delayed or Not Delivered*, WASH. POST, Oct. 20, 1994, at C3.

43. Questions Submitted to the Postmaster General by Chairman John H. McHugh Following the Postmaster General's Testimony of February 23, 1995, Subcommittee on the Postal Service, House Committee on Government Reform and Oversight 37 (May, 4, 1995).

44. *See* Jonathan M. Karpoff & John R. Lott, Jr., *The Reputational Penalty Firms Bear from Committing Criminal Fraud*, 36 J.L. & ECON. 757

criminal penalty or civil damage award.[45] Economists attribute this decrement of market value to a reputational penalty that the capital markets impose on the firm in the expectation that the occurrence in question may signal that the firm's future earnings may suffer as a result of further derelictions. Of course, no such barometer of the market value of the Postal Service exists, because it is wholly owned by the federal government. No fraction of the ownership of the Postal Service trades over a national exchange, and thus one cannot employ the familiar event-study methodology from corporate finance to evaluate the reputational harm to the Postal Service from revelations that its employees had stolen or destroyed mail or had knowingly failed to deliver it in a timely manner.

Private firms and the Postal Service differ in one other significant respect in terms of how they bear the costs of criminal wrongdoing or negligence by their employees. In a private firm, the harm to reputation is also borne individually by managers through diminished lifetime earnings resulting from their association with illegal or negligent conduct. In the Postal Service, however, there is at least anecdotal evidence that intentional misconduct by postal managers has failed to elicit significant penalties in terms of termination or demotion, let alone civil or criminal prosecution. For example, the article in *The New Yorker* reported that the mail processing director for Chicago

> had spent two hundred thousand dollars of [Postal Service] maintenance funds to refurbish her office suite with hardwood kitchen cabinets, a marble bathroom, and an air-conditioner for each of the suite's seven windows. Rumor has

---

(1993); Michael T. Maloney & Mark L. Mitchell, *Crisis in the Cockpit? The Role of Market Forces in Promoting Air Travel Safety*, 32 J.L. & ECON. 329 (1989).

45. Karpoff & Lott, *supra* note 44, at 796–97.

it that word of the renovation quite literally leaked out when water from [her] whirlpool bath came through the ceiling of the express-mail unit, two floors down.[46]

This postal manager was punished by being transferred, without any reduction in pay, to a suburban Chicago facility where her husband was the plant manager.[47]

Conclusion

Public provision of the full range of postal services is no longer necessary. The Postal Service is not a natural monopoly. The absence of insurmountable barriers to entry in postal delivery has allowed extensive provision of postal services on a competitive basis and will continue to enable private firms to provide additional mail services as regulation permits. In the absence of the Postal Service's statutory monopoly over letter mail, one would observe competitive provision of all classes of mail service.

The contemporary rationales offered for continuing the public provision of the full range of postal services are (1) to ensure ubiquity of service and uniformity of pricing throughout the country and (2) to ensure the integrity of the mail stream. We have shown that private firms, whose managers are obliged to maximize profit for its shareholders, can be relied upon to a greater extent than the Postal Service to supply secure delivery of letters and parcels. Further, in the presence of a funding mechanism for universal service that is more sensible than the current method of rate averaging, public control of postal services would be unnecessary to ensure ubiquity of service and geographic uniformity of pric-

---

46. Franzen, *supra* note 36, at 72.
47. *Id.*

ing and quality. Therefore, the competitive provision of letter mail would not compromise universal service, and it would seem more likely to increase rather than decrease the integrity and efficiency of the mail stream because of the superior incentive structures facing managers in private firms.

5
Overseeing the Postal Monopoly

PUBLIC CONTROL of the Postal Service has four main components: regulatory control, managerial control, congressional oversight, and executive branch oversight. Taken together, those components differ substantially from traditional utility regulation because they inject political considerations into the management of the Postal Service. Public control as currently established involves multiple supervisors who are pursuing different and at times conflicting objectives. Almost inevitably, the result of such a complex and politicized process is a departure from economic efficiency in the attempt to please everyone.

Through its enactment of the Postal Reorganization Act of 1970, Congress transformed the Post Office Department from a cabinet-level agency into the current Postal Service.[1]

---

1. Postal Reorganization Act, Pub. L. No. 91-375, 84 Stat. 719 (1970). For a thorough analysis of the legislation, see William Ty Mayton, *The Mission and Methods of the Postal Service, in* GOVERNING THE POSTAL SERVICE 60 (J. Gregory Sidak ed., AEI Press 1994).

Although Congress intended postal reorganization to make the Post Office more businesslike and to insulate it from political influence, the legislation failed to alter the public ownership of the Post Office. Nor did the legislation subject the Postal Service to the legal obligations of a private firm. Instead, the new Postal Service was to be a government-owned enterprise that inherited the privileges of the old Post Office, subject to the regulatory oversight of a new Postal Rate Commission—an organization that even in 1995 had only fifty employees, including its five commissioners[2]—which experience would subsequently reveal to be largely ineffectual for legal and political reasons.[3]

Our criticism of public control of the Postal Service is *not* a recommendation to eliminate the Postal Rate Commission. To the contrary, some public control of the Postal Service is necessary for as long as the Postal Service continues to enjoy a statutory monopoly over letter mail. If the Private Express Statutes were repealed, and if the antitrust laws were enforced against the Postal Service, then, following a transitional period, it would be possible to abolish the Postal Rate Commission. Until that time, however, an effective regulatory check on the Postal Service is essential.

REGULATORY CONTROL

The Postal Rate Commission reviews rates of the Postal Service in a manner similar to that of a state public utility commission, with public rate hearings. The Postal Rate

---

2. *Hearings Before the Subcomm. on the Postal Service of the House Comm. on Government Reform and Oversight*, 104th Cong., 1st Sess. (Mar. 2, 1995) (testimony of Edward J. Gleiman, Chairman, Postal Rate Commission).

3. *See* R. Richard Geddes, *Agency Costs and Governance in the United States Postal Service, in* GOVERNING THE POSTAL SERVICE, *supra* note 1, at 114, 129–33.

Commission's five commissioners are appointed by the President and confirmed by the Senate.[4] As with other regulatory commissions, the Postal Rate Commission holds a trial-type administrative hearing in which it gathers evidence, compiles a formal record, and recommends postal rates, subject to statutory restrictions contained in the Postal Reorganization Act. Market participants appearing before the Postal Rate Commission are entitled to due process under the Constitution.

There is a subtle but important difference between what due process means for utility regulation and what it means for postal regulation. In the case of utility regulation, due process protects not only ratepayers, but also the utility's shareholders. Investors are promised a fair or competitive rate of return on their capital. As Justice Douglas stated in *Federal Power Commission* v. *Hope Natural Gas Co.* in 1944, "[t]he rate-making process under the [Natural Gas] Act; *i.e.*, the fixing of 'just and reasonable' rates, involves a balancing of the investor and consumer interests."[5] In contrast, the Postal Service, being publicly owned and prohibited from making a profit, has no investor interests comparable to those of a private firm. In that respect, the due process protections in postal regulation are inevitably reserved for other interests and can be seen to perform a function similar to the consumer welfare standard in antitrust law.[6]

The Postal Reorganization Act specifies, in section 3622(b), eight criteria for ratemaking. In addition to taking into account "other factors that it deems appropriate," the

---

4. 39 U.S.C. § 3601(a).

5. 320 U.S. 591, 603 (1944). *See also* Bluefield Waterworks & Improvement Co. *v.* Public Serv. Comm'n, 262 U.S. 679 (1923).

6. *See, e.g.*, National Collegiate Athletic Ass'n *v.* Board of Regents of Univ. of Okla., 468 U.S. 85, 107 (1984); Reiter *v.* Sonotone Corp., 442 U.S. 330, 343 (1979) (citing ROBERT H. BORK, THE ANTITRUST PARADOX: A POLICY AT WAR WITH ITSELF 66 (Free Press 1978)).

Postal Rate Commission must take into account the interests of market participants *other than the Postal Service*.[7] The remaining six criteria include: fair and equitable rates; the value of the mail to the sender and the recipient; the effect of rate increases on the general public, business mail users, and private sector carriers of mail other than letters; the alternative means of sending mail; the degree of preparation of the mail by the mailer; and simplicity of the rate structure.[8]

Only indirectly does the statute address the interests of the Postal Service itself. The extent to which the shipper's preparation of the mail reduces the costs of the Postal Service should be reflected in rates, presumably through discounts. In addition, the Postal Rate Commission must take into account "the requirement that each class of mail or type of mail service bear the direct and indirect postal costs attributable to that class or type plus that portion of all other costs of the Postal Service reasonably assignable to such class or type."[9] That provision summarizes the cost-based nature of Postal Service ratemaking and refers to both cost recovery (the regulatory revenue requirement) and cost allocation (the regulatory rate structure).

Because utility regulation and postal regulation are both based on the recovery of costs that are measured in accordance with accounting standards, one can argue that there is little quantitative difference between the two. That is not the case, however. The main difference between utility regulation and postal regulation is that the Postal Service and the Postal Rate Commission are not concerned with the provision of a competitive return to capital investment, because the Postal Service has no private shareholders. The information reporting requirements of the Postal Service are not so stringent as those of a regulated utility, and such scanty reporting

---

7. 39 U.S.C. § 3622(b)(4).
8. *Id.* § 3622(b).
9. *Id.* § 3622(b)(3).

has provoked controversy.

The Postal Rate Commission indirectly controls the nonpublic segments of postal markets because the Postal Service competes directly with companies providing parcel post and express mail. Indeed, the inverse elasticity pricing advocated by the GAO, the postmaster general, and the Postal Service is specifically intended to improve the Postal Service's position relative to its competitors. Regarding parcel post and express mail, the GAO states that "the Postal Service is unlikely to gain ground on its competitors unless it can offer competitive prices."[10] The implications of that statement are evident from the GAO report. By instituting value-of-service pricing, the Postal Service can increase its market share at the expense of its competitors. Without question, the diversion of business from private companies by a public enterprise is tantamount to government regulation of competitive markets. The regulatory constraint is binding if the public enterprise offers a competitively priced alternative, although clearly such regulation takes a different form from traditional regulation of public utilities.

The de facto regulation of private firms by the Postal Rate Commission raises serious questions of law and economic policy. There is no evidence of market failure of any sort in the markets for parcel delivery and overnight mail. To the contrary, those markets are manifestly competitive for the reasons described in chapter 3. Nonetheless, in each market the price that the Postal Rate Commission sets for the Postal Service imposes constraints, on a quality-adjusted basis, on the prices of private competitors such as Federal Express and United Parcel Service. Some postal analysts actually applaud that result on the ground that it constrains the exercise of market power in what they assert to be an oligopolistic indus-

---

10. GENERAL ACCOUNTING OFFICE, U.S. POSTAL PRICING: PRICING POSTAL SERVICES IN A COMPETITIVE ENVIRONMENT 5 (1992) [hereinafter GAO REPORT].

try.[11] Even if one accepts for sake of argument that the market is an oligopoly, that reasoning is unpersuasive. The Federal Trade Commission and the Antitrust Division of the Department of Justice already exist to police competition in the overnight mail and parcel delivery markets. Further, as a legal matter, Congress empowered the Postal Rate Commission to regulate the Postal Service, *not* private providers of competitive mail services.

Managerial Control

Because the Postal Service is a publicly owned enterprise, its owners are the American people. Unlike shareholders in a privately owned corporation, however, the owners of the Postal Service have no claim to the residual net cash flows that the Postal Service generates from its operations.[12] Even if the Postal Service generates a surplus, the owners receive no dividend. Moreover, they cannot sell their ownership claims; a given investor cannot aggregate ownership claims and reap a greater return to monitoring the Postal Service's economic performance. Finally, unlike most common stock, which confers voting rights along with rights to the firm's residual net cash flows, ownership of the Postal Service does not confer the ability to influence the governance of the Postal Service through any sort of proxy process.

A private firm maximizes profit because doing so maximizes the value of the firm for its shareholders. The Postal Service, however, does not maximize profit. Instead, it must be assumed to be maximizing something else, such as the number of its employees, post offices, routes, or pieces of

---

11. Rand Cositch & Gail Willette, *Regulation of Unregulated Firms: The Postal Service and UPS, in* Commercialization of Postal and Delivery Services: National and International Perspectives 237 (Michael A. Crew & Paul R. Kleindorfer eds., Kluwer Academic Publishers 1994).

12. *See* Geddes, *supra* note 3, at 114, 116–17.

mail handled.[13] That condition implies, first, that the Postal Service is not using resources efficiently and minimizing cost. Second, it implies that a private firm, which does maximize profit, will likely find it difficult to compete against the Postal Service, particularly in the presence of cross-subsidization. Finally, the absence of a profit motive implies that, unlike a private firm, the Postal Service will not divest itself of product lines that are not economically viable. Without question, any private firm that has lost as much market share as the Postal Service has in parcel post and express mail would have contemplated divesting those product lines. Instead, the Postal Service is advocating the adoption of pricing policies intended to facilitate its expansion in those product lines, in part through the increased ability to cross-subsidize.

The Postal Reorganization Act of 1970 was designed not only to reform the Postal Service, but also to grant greater autonomy to its managers, particularly regarding financing, personnel, and administration.[14] A quarter century later, Postal Service managers are again seeking reform to achieve greater autonomy. The reorganization advocated in 1995 by Postmaster General Marvin Runyon, however, would loosen regulatory controls and oversight without removing the Postal Service's protection from market competition.

The Postal Service is overseen by an eleven-member board of governors,[15] which has the authority to override the

---

13. More formally, the alternative hypotheses include (1) maximization of consumer welfare subject to a minimum income constraint, (2) maximization of size (or output) with no income constraint, (3) maximization of size (or output) with an income constraint, and (4) maximization of employment.

14. *See* JOHN T. TIERNEY, THE U.S. POSTAL SERVICE: STATUS AND PROSPECTS OF A PUBLIC ENTERPRISE 29 (Auburn House 1988); Geddes, *supra* note 3, at 114, 129-38; Sharon M. Oster, *The Postal Service as a Public Enterprise, in id.* at 31; Mayton, *supra* note 1, at 85-109; Sharon M. Oster, *The Failure of Postal Reform*, 4 HUME PAPERS ON PUB. POL'Y (forthcoming 1995).

15. 39 U.S.C. § 201(a).

Postal Rate Commission's rate recommendations.[16] "It hardly seems appropriate," John Tierney has observed, "that a government agency enjoying a monopoly over certain of its services has the ultimate power to put into effect whatever rates it chooses."[17] Therefore, while ostensibly monitored by the Postal Rate Commission, the Postal Service and its board are effectively independent of regulatory control.

The board of governors exercises authority over the management of the Postal Service, but the objectives of its members are poorly defined. Private regulated utilities are subject to the control of a board of directors who ensure that the company's management represents the interests of the company's shareholders by maximizing the company's value. Because the Postal Service is a public enterprise, however, the board cannot be expected to maximize the value of the business. The board also cannot be said to act "in the public interest" because the interests of mailers differ considerably. In short, the board's mission and incentives are ill-defined because the objectives of the Postal Service are themselves ambiguous.

Because they oversee a public enterprise, the managers of the Postal Service exercise authority delegated to them by the U.S. government. Therefore, one might expect the management of the Postal Service to act in the government's interest, just as managers of private companies are expected to act in their shareholders' interests. The government's interests, however, are difficult to define. They can be expected to reflect not only the preferences of the bureaucracy, but also the preferences of influential groups that participate in the regulatory process, the Postal Rate Commission, the executive branch, and Congress.

---

16. *Id.* § 3625(a).
17. TIERNEY, *supra* note 14, at 210.

Postal Service management monitors its own economic performance. The postmaster general and the deputy postmaster general sit on the board of governors and thus further blur the line between monitors and management. The Postal Rate Commission does not directly monitor cost efficiency. Internal accounting, production, and demand information on the Postal Service is difficult to obtain and interpret. For example, the Postal Rate Commission noted in its 1991 rate decision: "The continued reliance of Postal Service witnesses on unusual and ad hoc estimation techniques in place of generally accepted methods has made it impossible for the Commission to assess the statistical properties of the Service's volume and revenue forecasts."[18] In an organization without clearly defined objectives and lacking independent monitoring, managers would be expected to pursue personal objectives such as increased authority, increased remuneration, or reduced responsibility. The existing system of public control is diametrically opposed to the performance incentives faced by managers of private firms. Increasing managerial autonomy can only worsen the present state of affairs.

What are the financial objectives of the Postal Service? The Postal Service has a "revenue requirement." Its objective ostensibly is to break even. On each unit of mail it handles, the Postal Service earns a contribution to the recovery of its common fixed costs. In this respect, the Postal Service does not have a "profit margin." Conceivably, however, if the demand for mail in a given year exceeded the volumes projected by the Postal Service, revenues might exceed costs incurred for that year. One might expect that surplus to revert to the federal government under the Miscellaneous Receipts

---

18. Postal Rate and Fee Changes, 1990, Opinion and Recommended Decision, vol. 1, Dkt. No. R90-1, at II-71 ¶ 2133 (Postal Rate Commission 1991).

Act[19] as part of the general revenues. To the contrary, surplus funds earned by the Postal Service in any fixed year are deposited with the Treasury in a fund available to the Postal Service.[20] The Treasury invests those funds on behalf of the Postal Service, and the Postal Service may draw them down to pay expenses in future years. Because the Postal Service includes in institutional costs the recovery of prior years' losses, which the Postal Service estimated to have a cumulative value of $8.425 billion at the end of fiscal year 1994,[21] a "profit" earned in the current fiscal year may simply recover a larger share of earlier losses and thus defer a further rate increase, which the Postal Service's management may value.

The current postmaster general believes that the Postal Service should be a "profit center" for the federal government, but what this means is unclear in light of the fact that the Postal Service is subject to a break-even revenue requirement and does not earn "profit." Indeed, the Postal Service has almost invariably incurred losses since postal reorganization. One interpretation of the postmaster general's remark is that the government should retain the monopoly rents earned as a result of the regulatory barriers to entry into delivery of letter mail. That situation is little more than a disguised tax on postal delivery. Unlike competitive markets, where economic profits—that is, profits beyond what is necessary to pay investors a competitive return on capital—provide incentives for entry and innovation, the profits earned by a protected public enterprise have no such incentive effects. The Postal Service may have an incentive to earn revenues that cover its costs, to give the impression that it is efficiently managed, but there is no incentive for managers to reduce costs. In that respect,

---

19. Act of Mar. 3, 1849, ch. 110, 9 Stat. 398 (codified as amended at 31 U.S.C. § 3302(b)).

20. 39 U.S.C. §§ 2003, 2006.

21. Postal Rate and Fee Changes, 1994, Opinion and Recommended Decision, Dkt. No. R94-1, at II-16 ¶ 2049 (Postal Rate Commission 1994).

economic profits earned by the Postal Service may simply be dissipated by escalating costs or by uneconomic investments to enter new markets.

Some might argue that the sheer inefficiency of the Postal Service precludes it from engaging in predation against private firms. That argument is incorrect, however, for the Postal Service's misallocation of costs to first class mail —however bloated those costs may be—can enable it to price in a manner that would be predatory under the established antitrust standard. The possibility that the Postal Service would spare no expense to expand its market share is precisely the reason for limiting the lines of business in which the Postal Service may operate.

To the extent that monitoring is limited, Postal Service managers can be expected to pursue personal objectives. Such a course of action need not take the form of salary increases or perquisites. What is more likely is that the managers will seek to expand the Postal Service through growth in mail volume and diversification into other lines of business. Managers can represent a greater volume of mail as a sign of success. Managers can interpret greater demand for the Postal Service's services as evidence that it serves an economically useful function. By handling more pieces of mail, the Postal Service can justify increasing both employment and investment expenditures. That, in turn, increases the authority of managers by expanding the number of subordinates who report to them. Managers also can attain a sense of greater importance and take satisfaction from supervising a business with high revenues. Finally, increased volumes of mail reduce the unit-cost impact of overhead expenditures and allow postal management costs to expand or at least to avoid the severe downsizing undertaken by many competitive firms.

The Postal Service can achieve greater growth by expanding operations in parcel post and express mail. The managers of the Postal Service are campaigning for increased flexibility to carry out such diversification. As a consequence of inelastic demand in first class and third class mail, due in part to the statutory postal monopoly, price increases will have a relatively low impact on mail volume in those categories. In contrast, price reductions in parcel post and express mail could yield substantial increases in volume to the extent that the Postal Service increases the amount demanded and diverts market share from competitive companies.

Managers of private companies also have incentives to achieve higher growth rates and to compete for market share. Unlike the managers of the Postal Service, however, they cannot pursue those objectives independently of profit maximization objectives. Companies that offer discounts to build market share do so in anticipation of economic returns from future sales. The managers of the Postal Service do not operate under such constraints.

Indeed, because the Postal Service is a public enterprise, it is subject to considerable political influence. It faces public pressure to increase or maintain employment, and it has an incentive to increase wages to satisfy labor unions. Since the Postal Service is not a profit-maximizing institution, it need not minimize operating costs, including wages and salaries. The Postal Service is structured in a manner that increases the bargaining power of labor unions. The Postal Reorganization Act established an independent personnel system that allows management to engage in direct collective bargaining with unions.[22] That arrangement resulted in substantial wage premiums for Postal Service workers in comparison with competitive rates.[23]

---

22. TIERNEY, *supra* note 14, at 28.

23. After the reorganization, postal salaries were 21 percent higher than competitive rates. Douglas K. Adie, *How Have the Postal Workers Fared Since the 1970 Act?, in* PERSPECTIVES ON POSTAL SERVICE ISSUES 74 (Roger Sherman ed., AEI Press 1980). George Priest has subsequently observed that the Postal Service has the largest unionized work force in the country, and that it is one of the few organizations in which union membership has grown

In addition, the Postal Service has an interest in increasing capital and equipment costs by maintaining post offices in congressional districts. By statute, the closing of any post office must be preceded by public notice, and the decision to close is appealable to the Postal Rate Commission.[24] The Postal Reorganization Act also grants the Postal Service the authority to borrow money and issue bonds.[25] The Postal Service's investment decisions are not influenced by the costs of labor and capital in the same manner as those of a competitive private enterprise.

Congressional Oversight

The Senate exercises oversight of the Postal Service through the confirmation process for presidential appointments to its board of governors. Congress further exercises oversight through appropriations for explicitly subsidized services, which have been gradually phased out;[26] through oversight hearings concerning the Postal Rate Commission; through legislation affecting the organization of the Postal Service, such as the Postal Reorganization Act of 1970; and through studies prepared by the General Accounting Office.

Congressional oversight occurs in another manner that, while indirect and informal, will tend to be solicitous to the interests of the Postal Service. Given the electoral significance of an organization with 850,000 employees, it is natural to expect that the congressional committees overseeing the Postal Service would sympathize with the interests of the Postal Service and its unionized work force to a greater extent than

---

rather than declined. George L. Priest, *Socialism, Eastern Europe, and the Question of the Postal Monopoly, in* Governing the Postal Service, *supra* note 1, at 46, 51.
   24. 39 U.S.C. § 404(b).
   25. *Id.* § 2005.
   26. *Id.* § 2401(b).

with the interests of the Postal Service's customers or private competitors.

EXECUTIVE BRANCH OVERSIGHT

The President exercises some influence over the Postal Service through his appointments to the board of governors. But as the long line of cases and the enormous body of academic writing associated with *Humphrey's Executor* make clear, the President's power to remove officers may be a more important tool of oversight than his power to appoint them.[27] On this score, executive branch oversight of the Postal Service is weak indeed.

In January 1993 President Bush threatened to remove certain members of the board of governors unless they dropped a lawsuit challenging the Postal Rate Commission's recommendation for a two-cent discount for bar-coded, machine-processed first class mail.[28] President Bush favored the recommendation and argued that the Postal Service could not litigate a case if the Department of Justice disapproved. A federal district judge preliminarily enjoined President Bush from firing the governors.[29] When President Bush nevertheless attempted to remove one governor and make a recess appointment of a new one, the judge ruled that the President lacks such removal power.[30] A subsequent court decision nullified the recess appointment.[31] Meanwhile, the U.S. Court of Ap-

---

27. Humphrey's Executor v. United States, 295 U.S. 602 (1935).

28. *See* Neal Devins, *Tempest in an Envelope: Reflections on the Bush White House's Failed Takeover of the U.S. Postal Service,* 41 UCLA L. REV. 1035 (1994); Geddes, *supra* note 3, at 132–33; *Bush Reportedly Threatens Postal Board over Rate Rise,* N.Y. TIMES, Jan. 5, 1993, at A11.

29. Mackie v. Bush, 809 F. Supp. 144 (D.D.C. 1993); *Bush Temporarily Prevented from Dismissing Postmaster,* N.Y. TIMES, Jan. 8, 1993, at A13.

30. *Court Blocks Dismissal of Postal Governors,* N.Y. TIMES, Jan. 17, 1993, at I22.

31. Mackie v. Clinton, 827 F. Supp. 56 (D.D.C. 1993).

peals for the District of Columbia Circuit ruled that the Postal Service could indeed litigate independently of the Department of Justice.[32] As a practical matter, therefore, no credible threat backs the executive branch's oversight of the Postal Service.

Conclusion

The Postal Service is not subject to effective oversight by the Postal Rate Commission, by the board of governors, by Congress, or by the President. Despite this condition, the postmaster general has said in May 1995 that "too many other people" than the management of the Postal Service "have too much say in the price [that postal customers] pay."[33] The problems, in his view, are "taxes," regulators, and competitors:

> From 1987 through 1998, the Government has assessed us $14 billion, a stamp tax to help reduce the federal deficit. A dozen agencies and organizations oversee parts of our business. Competitors help set postage rates. They get access to sensitive business information. And they push for higher prices for us, so they can raise theirs.[34]

Taxes, regulators, and competitors are, of course, the usual

---

32. Mail Order Ass'n v. United States Postal Serv., 986 F.2d 509 (D.C. Cir. 1993).

33. Address by Postmaster General Marvin Runyon to the National Postal Forum, Nashville, Tennessee 3 (May 8, 1995).

34. *Id.* at 3–4. Of course, the Postal Service does not pay any federal or state income taxes. The postmaster general's reference to "taxes" refers to legislation in which Congress required the Postal Service rather than taxpayers to pay the costs of certain postal employee benefits.

irritants that any private firm must endure. Given the privileges and immunities already enjoyed by the Postal Service, especially its monopoly under the Private Express Statutes, it is telling that the postmaster general would criticize the current oversight of Postal Service pricing by saying, "You cannot survive, much less compete, unless you control your prices."[35] It is standard antitrust doctrine that unconstrained monopoly power is defined as "the power to control market prices or exclude competition."[36] The postmaster general's remarks may therefore be read to express a desire to obtain the same species of unregulated power in the marketplace that the Sherman Act exists to prevent private firms from acquiring or exploiting.

Four days before making the preceding remarks, the postmaster general even more explicitly expressed his desire to rid his pricing decisions of any public oversight. In response to questions from members of the House Subcommittee on the Postal Service, he provided the following written statement:

> [QUESTION:] I know that as a businessman you have strong views regarding the Postal Rate Commission and the restrictions the present ratemaking process places on your abilities to compete. However, I would like you to elaborate on how postal customers would be protected without the Postal Rate Comission and its proceedings.
>
> ANSWER: If, hypothetically, the Postal Rate Commission were eliminated from the ratemaking process, it should still be possible to

---

35. *Id.* at 3.
36. United States *v.* E.I. du Pont de Nemours & Co., 351 U.S. 377, 391 (1956).

protect the interests of postal customers. It should be recognized that the Governors of the Postal Service are appointed to serve the public interest generally, and are not to be representatives of any specific interests using the Postal Service. As their compensation is set by statute, they have no financial incentive to pursue any interests other than the one they were appointed to serve. The Postal Service is unaware of any other reason why they would fail to fulfill their duty. It is therefore unclear why there is any perceived need to protect postal customers beyond the oversight of the Governors.

If, however, some other form of institutional protection were desired, it need not involve the anomaly of having one executive branch body regulate another. In its 1968 report, to cite one example, the Kappel Commission recommended that rate proposals be evaluated by an internal body of technical examiners responsible only to the directors of the postal corporation. The postal directors would then have acted on the recommendations of the technical panel, subject to disapproval by a concurrent resolution of Congress. I am sure that other, even more creative ways might be found to safeguard the interests of postal customers in a restructured ratemaking process.[37]

The most charitable commentary that can be made on these remarks by the postmaster general is that they reveal profound

---

37. Questions Submitted to the Postmaster General by Chairman John M. McHugh Following the Postmaster General's Testimony of February 23, 1995, Subcommittee on the Postal Service, House Committee on Government Reform and Oversight 17 (May 4, 1995).

naiveté about the manner in which ostensibly disinterested regulatory institutions respond to the demands of interest groups. A less charitable commentary is that those remarks document a monopolist's desire to be its own regulator.

Public control of the Postal Service is necessary for as long as it retains a monopoly over letter mail under the Private Express Statutes. Unfortunately, the current forms of public control of the Postal Service are ineffectual. In essence, the Postal Service is an unregulated monopolist that is constrained only in the sense that it is expedient for the enterprise not to show a profit. Consequently, the Postal Service has an incentive to reap monopoly rents from captive customers and then dissipate those rents by investing in new lines of business of questionable relevance to the Postal Service's traditional mission under the Postal Reorganization Act to deliver letter mail.

6

The Competitive Problems of Postal Service Pricing and Regulations

UNLIKE A PRIVATE FIRM in a regulated industry, the Postal Service is not subject to the demanding oversight of a state public utility commission or federal regulatory agency. From a competitive perspective, the principal harm that regulatory oversight can prevent is the misallocation of costs by the Postal Service from competitive classes of mail to letter mail, which is protected by a statutory monopoly.

PREVENTING ANTICOMPETITIVE COST MISALLOCATION BY THE POSTAL SERVICE

In regulated private industries one way of reducing the incentive and opportunity for anticompetitive cross-subsidization is to replace cost-of-service regulation with price caps.[1] The

---

1. *See* BRIDGER M. MITCHELL & INGO VOGELSANG, TELECOMMUNICATIONS PRICING: THEORY AND PRACTICE 167–75, 276–85 (Cambridge Univer-

Postal Service, however, is not subject to price caps. Moreover, it is doubtful that price caps would even be feasible for the Postal Service.

The Logic of Price Caps

Price caps resemble the phenomenon of regulatory lag—that is, the general delay in the responses of regulators to changes in cost or market conditions. In addition, price caps may allow the firm pricing flexibility and can reduce the administrative cost of rate hearings.

Suppose that the firm's prices are set on the basis of current costs, and the firm succeeds in reducing those costs substantially. Suppose further that, say, two years elapse before regulators require the firm to cut its prices correspondingly. Then the firm will enjoy two years of superior profits as its reward for improved efficiency. That process mimics a competitive market, where a cost-cutting innovator enjoys superior but temporary profits. Those higher profits end when rivals introduce their own cost-reducing innovations and wipe out the competitive advantage temporarily enjoyed by the earlier innovator.

The built-in regulatory lag at the heart of the price-cap approach must be substantial, because otherwise firms will have no effective incentive to undertake the heavy costs and risks of innovation, and society will be the loser. On the other hand, the lag, like the life of a patent, must not be infinite, lest the consuming public be forced to forgo the benefits of

---

sity Press 1991); Ronald R. Braeutigam & John C. Panzar, *Effects of the Change from Rate-of-Return to Price-Cap Regulation*, 83 AM. ECON. REV. PAPERS & PROC. 191 (1993); Ronald R. Braeutigam & John C. Panzar, *Diversification Incentives Under "Price-Based" and "Cost-Based" Regulation*, 20 RAND J. ECON. 373, 387–90 (1989); Tracy R. Lewis & David E. M. Sappington, *Regulatory Options and Price Cap Regulation*, 20 RAND J. ECON. 405 (1989).

lower prices that the competitive market normally transmits to it.

Regulatory lag thus supplies the incentive required to elicit innovation and productivity growth, with one critical exception. When inflation is substantial, regulatory lag delays the adjustment of output prices to compensate for inflationary increases in nominal input costs. That delay squeezes the profits of the regulated firm and undercuts both its incentive and its ability to invest in innovation. To deal with the inflation problem, the price-cap arrangement uses the following procedures. First, an initial price ceiling is determined on the basis of stand-alone cost or a defensible proxy. Second, the price ceiling is permitted to rise automatically each year by a percentage equal to the rise of some widely accepted index of inflation, such as the consumer price index (CPI), after subtracting some number, X, from the percentage increase in that price index. The arrangement is often referred to as "CPI − X." Third, X is calculated from the industry's differential rate of productivity growth in the past, or as a target rate of productivity growth for the industry.

The logic of price caps is straightforward: The firm is permitted a percentage increase in the profit margin on its product that precisely equals the amount by which its productivity performance exceeded the target. The opposite is experienced by a firm whose productivity performance falls short of the target. In sum, under price caps, the firm whose productivity increase exceeds the norm will enjoy higher returns exactly commensurate with its achievement, while the firm with poor productivity performance will automatically be penalized correspondingly.

Price caps do more than induce the private firm to minimize its cost of production. They also reduce the incentive for the firm to cross-subsidize new lines of business through the misallocation of costs, for the firm may charge up to its maximum price whether or not its accounting costs for the regulated service change. In that manner, price caps attenuate the link that rate-of-return regulation creates between the regulated firm's realized production costs and its allowed earnings. Under rate-of-return regulation, the firm can raise its allowed earnings whenever it can mischaracterize costs incurred in the production of unregulated products as having been incurred in the production of regulated products. Under price-cap regulation, however, the firm is not allowed higher revenues from regulated services when the costs of those specific activities rise; thus, the firm's ability to increase its earnings by assigning accounting costs from its unregulated services to its regulated services is decreased. This decreased ability to profit from cost misallocation correspondingly reduces the firm's incentive to attempt cross-subsidization.

Price Caps and the Postal Service

In contrast to a private firm subject to price caps, the Postal Service has both a large incentive and a good opportunity to engage in anticompetitive cross-subsidization. The Postal Service is not subject to any explicit price-cap regulation and its rate proceedings occur relatively quickly.[2] Indeed, the statutory requirement that the Postal Rate Commission issue recommended decisions in rate proceedings within ten months,[3] while desirable on grounds of administrative efficiency, incidentally contributes to the inability of postal rates to resemble price caps. Under such circumstances, not only is the Postal Service likely to allocate common fixed costs arbitrarily across classes of mail, but the Postal Service is more able than a regulated private firm (such as a local exchange carrier) to fail to attribute costs that can be causally traced to

---

2. For proposals to subject the Postal Service to price caps, see Michael A. Crew & Paul R. Kleindorfer, *Pricing, Entry, Service Quality, and Innovations Under a Commercialized Postal Service*, in GOVERNING THE POSTAL SERVICE 150, 161–67 (J. Gregory Sidak ed., AEI Press 1994).

3. 39 U.S.C. § 3624(c)(1).

a particular class of mail—particularly a class of mail, such as parcel post or overnight mail, for which the Postal Service experiences substantial competition. One would expect cost misallocation by the Postal Service to be an increasing function of the share of total costs that the Postal Service asserts that it cannot attribute to any particular class of mail.

Moreover, it is doubtful that price caps could work for the Postal Service.[4] The statutory requirement of revenue adequacy in the Postal Reorganization Act does not envision operating the enterprise on a for-profit basis. Consequently, the driving force that produces consumer benefits when price caps are applied to a privately owned firm—the firm's incentive to minimize costs and thereby increase profits—would be absent if price caps were applied to the Postal Service. Even if there were no legal requirement that the Postal Service operate on a break-even basis, both experience and economic theory strongly suggest that the management of this public enterprise does not attempt to maximize profit or minimize cost. If so, then the Postal Service would not respond to the incentives that price caps present.

Finally, postal rates are, by Postal Rate Commission regulations and arguably by statute[5] and legislative history, based on costs for a *future test year*, not on current or historical costs. That factor at least reduces, if it does not eliminate, the impact of regulatory lag.

Incorrect Measurement and Misallocation of Attributable Costs

The Postal Service has five major classes of mail: (1) letters and postcards, (2) newspapers and periodicals, (3) bulk busi-

---

4. *See* George R. Hall, *Regulatory Systems for Postal Rates, in* REGULATION AND THE NATURE OF POSTAL AND DELIVERY SERVICES 221 (Michael A. Crew & Paul R. Kleindorfer eds., Kluwer Academic Publishers 1993).

5. 39 U.S.C. § 3621 (referring to *estimated* costs and revenues).

ness mail, (4) parcels, and (5) express mail. Such product categories are an arbitrary segmentation of the mail market based on the characteristics of the mailer. The categories exist to facilitate regulatory ratemaking and do not necessarily conform to market segments that might be identified today for pricing and marketing purposes. Indeed, in March 1995 the Postal Service initiated a proceeding before the Postal Rate Commission to reclassify the mail.[6]

Cost-of-Service Regulation of the Postal Service

A competitive firm sets price on the basis of its costs, its customers' willingness to pay, and the anticipated prices that the firm's actual and potential competitors will charge for their products. Unlike competitive firms, a firm subject to rate-of-return regulation sets price on the basis of accounting measures of operating costs and capital expenditures, and the allowed rate-of-return on capital. In the case of the Postal Service, the Postal Rate Commission begins by determining the Postal Service's revenue requirement on the basis of projected levels of demand for the various classes of mail. Costs for a "test year" in the future are estimated on the basis of those estimated demand levels, expected inflation rate, and estimated productivity. If estimated total costs would exceed estimated revenues in the test year, using existing rates, the Postal Rate Commission recommends rate increases. The higher rates that would enable the Postal Service to break even reflect the fact that demand would fall (and hence total costs would change) as rates rise in accordance with the relevant price elasticities.

The prices established by a regulated firm that offers

---

6. Mail Classification Schedule, 1995, Classification Reform I, Dkt. No. MC 95-1 (Postal Rate Commission 1995).

multiple products and services, or that distinguishes between multiple customer classes, are referred to as its *rate structure*. After the Postal Rate Commission determines the Postal Service's revenue requirement, it addresses cost attribution and rate design. Each class must cover its attributable costs and make at least some contribution to the recovery of institutional costs. Understandably, great controversy surrounds the determination of whether a cost is attributable to a particular class of mail and how institutional costs should be apportioned among the various classes of mail.[7]

Tests for Cross-Subsidies in Multiproduct Firms

A break-even regulated rate structure is said to be free of cross-subsidies if and only if the prices satisfy the *stand-alone cost test*.[8] Stand-alone cost refers to the firm's long-run total

---

7. For a discussion of the mechanics of a Postal Rate Commission case, see Hall, *supra* note 4; Crew & Kleindorfer, *supra* note 2, at 160. Because the Postal Service has no shareholders, the form of cost-of-service regulation to which it is subject differs somewhat from the cost-of-service regulation applied to private firms:

> The testimony on the allowed rate of return, which is paramount in traditional utility regulation, is not part of postal rate hearings. If the utility regulator allows a higher rate of return, the stockholders potentially stand to benefit. In postal service regulation, however, there is not the same direct concern with rate of return. The Postal Service has a break-even requirement, which includes covering interest payments on its borrowing. The requirement to establish an opportunity cost of capital, the basis of most rate-of-return testimony in utility cases, is not present in postal rate cases.

Id. For a discussion of cost-of-service regulation of private firms, see DANIEL F. SPULBER, REGULATION AND MARKETS 271-79 (MIT Press 1989).

8. *See, e.g.,* WILLIAM J. BAUMOL & J. GREGORY SIDAK, TOWARD COMPETITION IN LOCAL TELEPHONY 81 (MIT Press & AEI Press 1994); WILLIAM

cost of each service operated separately. The stand-alone cost test requires that the revenues generated from either of two services not exceed the stand-alone cost of providing that service. If the revenues from one service do exceed its stand-alone cost while the revenues from the other service do not cover stand-alone costs, then the first service is providing a cross-subsidy to the other service.[9] The test for cross-subsidization demonstrates that the customers of the service providing the cross-subsidy would be better off if they could obtain that service independently of the other service.

A regulated firm's rate structure also can be said to be free of cross-subsidies if and only if the prices satisfy the *incremental cost test*, which is equivalent to the stand-alone cost test for a regulated rate structure.[10] When applying the incremental cost test, revenues generated by each service must cover the incremental cost of providing that service.[11] The rationale for the incremental cost test is the requirement that each service must generate revenues that at least cover the additional cost of producing that service. If not, the other service is providing a cross-subsidy, and the customers of the other service would be better off receiving their service independently, at its stand-alone cost.

If a firm is regulated, it is desirable to design a rate structure that is free of cross-subsidies. Otherwise, the eco-

---

J. BAUMOL, JOHN C. PANZAR & ROBERT D. WILLIG, CONTESTABLE MARKETS AND THE THEORY OF INDUSTRY STRUCTURE 352–53 (Harcourt Brace Jovanovich 1982; rev. ed. 1988).

9. The definition of the stand-alone cost test is given in terms of two services. In the case of more than two services, the test requires that no group of services subsidize any other group of services.

10. *See* BAUMOL & SIDAK, *supra* note 8, at 57, 81–83; WILLIAM J. BAUMOL, SUPERFAIRNESS: APPLICATIONS AND THEORY 113–20 (MIT Press 1986).

11. The incremental cost test is defined here for only two services. In the case of more than two services, the revenues generated by each group of services must cover the incremental cost of providing that group of services.

nomic incentives can lead to allocative inefficiency. Customers receiving the subsidy do not observe the full economic costs of their service and consequently demand an inefficiently high amount; customers providing the subsidy demand an inefficiently low amount or seek bypass alternatives that may be uneconomic under some conditions.

The Postal Service's rate structure includes various types of cross-subsidies. One method of cross-subsidization is by uniform pricing of postal delivery regardless of origin or destination. Another method is through inappropriate accounting rules that misallocate costs, because the Postal Service is subject to cost-based rate regulation. The differences in transportation and delivery costs thus are not reflected in the postal rates. Since postal rates are set to enable the Postal Service to break even, it follows that some mailers are subsidizing others. Other types of explicit subsidies exist, including franking privileges and targeted discounts.

Attributable Costs and Institutional Costs

Putting aside explicit discounts, the method by which the Postal Rate Commission recommends postal rates may contain a number of implicit cross-subsidies. Those types of cross-subsidies result from incorrect measurement of costs. We distinguish two types of costs: *attributable costs*, which can be identified with the costs of specific services, and *institutional costs*, which refer to joint and common costs that cannot be attributed to any specific service.

Attributable costs generally are variable or "volume-sensitive" costs, such as labor and vehicles that can be assigned to specific types of sorting, collection, or delivery. Attributable costs also include fixed costs specifically incurred for particular types of mail. Institutional costs are fixed overhead and capital costs that are not volume-sensitive and do not correspond to any specific sorting, collection, or delivery activities. If attributable costs are correctly determined and prices for each service reflect those costs, arbitrary allocations of joint and common costs (that is, institutional costs) yield subsidy-free rate structures.[12] This proposition means that there is generally a wide range of subsidy-free rate structures. If regulators incorrectly classify some attributable costs as institutional costs, however, then accounting rules for allocating indirect costs can easily produce cross-subsidization. For example, until the Postal Rate Commission disapproved the practice in 1979, the Postal Service characterized advertising expenses for express mail as institutional costs rather than attributable costs of that particular service offering.[13]

To see the extent to which costs are shifted to the institutional category, consider table 6-1, which reproduces the Postal Service's own classification of costs among its twenty cost segements.[14] Although institutional costs are 39 percent of total costs, they are considerably greater in some categories. For example, it appears that while the "office activity" of city delivery carriers (cost segment 6) is only 10.1 percent institutional cost, their "street activity" (cost segment 7) is 71.1 percent institutional cost. The cost of rural carriers (cost segment 10) is 60.8 percent institutional cost. The implication of those numbers is that neither of the latter two categories is volume-sensitive and that neither category incurs any fixed cost specific to any particular type of mail. All fixed costs related to those activities are therefore institutional. Those implications seem to be at variance with the nature of the productive activities.

In fact, of the twenty Postal Service cost segments,

---

12. SPULBER, *supra* note 7, at 129.

13. Opinion and Recommended Decision, vol. 2, Dkt. No. R80-1, App. J at 256–57 ¶¶ 398–402 (Postal Rate Commission 1981) (discussing 1979 proceeding).

14. U.S. POSTAL SERVICE, SUMMARY DESCRIPTION OF USPS DEVELOPMENT OF COSTS BY SEGMENTS AND COMPONENTS, table 2, at xi (Dec. 1994) [hereinafter COSTS BY SEGMENTS AND COMPONENTS].

sixteen have *no specific fixed costs*, and three have *insignificant* specific fixed costs. The one remaining category, "other accrued expenses" (cost segment 20), has only 4.9 percent specific fixed costs, mostly for equipment depreciation; but even here, 38.8 percent of costs are institutional. In other words, the Postal Service recognizes practically no category-specific fixed costs. Therefore, almost all fixed costs are treated as joint and common costs under the institutional cost label. Such a categorization of costs is difficult to believe. How can almost 40 percent of total cost be joint and common fixed cost while not even 1 percent of total cost is category-specific? In other words, while the Postal Service's estimates of its fixed costs are high, virtually all of those fixed costs are incurred jointly across multiple cost categories, rather than being incurred on a segment-specific basis. (Of course, those cost categories do not correspond to product lines. Analysis of cost allocation by product line would shed further light on the likelihood of cross-subsidies between products.)

A possible explanation of this phenomenon might be that the "cost driver" selected by the Postal Service is not the appropriate measure of the sensitivity of costs to the economic activity. The Postal Service divides its twenty cost segments into about sixty-five cost components and 100 subcomponents.[15] For each cost element, the Postal Service identifies a "cost driver" that in its opinion "reflects the essential activity of that element."[16] For example, "carrier access costs are driven by the number of stops made by the letter carrier to deliver mail, and carrier 'load' costs are driven by pieces of each mail shape that a letter carrier loads into [a] mail receptacle."[17] The Postal Service calculates an "elasticity of cost" known as the "volume variability" of the cost. The elasticity

---

15. *Id.*, App. H (Calculating Postal Product Costs).
16. *Id.* at H-5.
17. *Id.* at H-4.

TABLE 6-1

PERCENTAGE SUMMARY OF FY 1993 COSTS BY COST SEGMENT AND CLASSIFICATION

		Attributable Costs			
Cost Segment	Total Accrued	Total	Total Volume-Variable	Specific-Fixed	Institutional
1. Postmasters	100.0	17.8	17.8	—	82.2
2. Supervisors and Technical Personnel	100.0	54.8	54.8	—	45.2
3. Clerks & Mailhandlers, CAG A-J Post Offices	100.0	87.2	86.7	.5	12.8
4. Clerks, CAG K Post Offices	100.0	60.2	60.2	—	39.8
5. (Segment Reserved)	—	—	—	—	—
6. City Delivery Carriers, Office Activity	100.0	89.9	89.9	—	10.1
7. City Delivery Carriers, Street Activity	100.0	28.9	28.9	—	71.1
8. Vehicle Service Drivers	100.0	47.3	47.3	—	52.7
9. Special Delivery Messengers	100.0	52.4	52.4	—	47.6
10. Rural Carriers	100.0	39.2	39.2	—	60.8
11. Custodial and Maintenance Services	100.0	62.2	62.2	—	37.8

TABLE 6-1 (CONTINUED)

PERCENTAGE SUMMARY OF FY 1993 COSTS BY COST SEGMENT AND CLASSIFICATION

| Cost Segment | Total Accrued | Attributable Costs ||||
		Total	Total Volume-Variable	Specific-Fixed	Institutional
12. Motor Vehicle Service	100.0	20.1	20.1	—	79.9
13. Miscellaneous Operating Costs	100.0	2.9	2.9	—	97.1
14. Purchased Transportation	100.0	86.5	86.5	—	13.5
15. Building Occupancy Costs	100.0	70.2	70.2	—	29.8
16. Supplies and Services	100.0	58.8	56.8	2.0	41.2
17. Research, Development, and Engineering	100.0	—	—	—	100.0
18. Administration and Regional Operations	100.0	35.3	35.2	.1	64.7
19. General Management Services	100.0	—	—	—	100.0
20. Other Accrued Services	100.0	61.2	56.3	4.9	38.8
Total	100.0	61.0	60.7	.3	39.0

SOURCE: COSTS BY SEGMENTS AND COMPONENTS, *supra* note 14, table 2, at xi.

of cost is the percentage change in cost divided by the percentage change in volume that "causes" the cost to increase. Then, the Postal Service estimates marginal cost by multiplying the total cost of the class by the elasticity of cost and dividing by volume. That computation estimates the change in cost for a change in volume. Attributable costs are calculated by multiplying marginal cost times volume and adding any specific fixed cost.[18]

The product of marginal cost times output, however, is an imperfect measure of variable cost. Suppose, for example, that variable costs are given by a quadratic function,

$$C(Q) = Q^2,$$

so that marginal cost equals $2Q$. Then, the product of marginal cost and volume is $MC \times Q = 2Q^2 = 2C(Q)$. This approach doubles the level of variable cost. Suppose instead that variable costs exhibit some economies of scale,

$$C(Q) = Q^{1/2},$$

so that marginal cost equals $.5Q^{-1/2}$. Then, the product of marginal cost and volume is $MC \times Q = .5Q^{1/2} = .5C(Q)$, which cuts in half the level of variable cost. Clearly, different specifications of the variable cost function can lead to significant errors in estimating attributable cost, even if marginal cost can be estimated accurately.[19]

The Postal Service uses several methods to calculate the attributable cost of a product. One approach, the "volume-variability" method, assigns costs on the basis of the "cost

---

18. *Id.* at H-3.
19. The Postal Service recognizes this problem in calculating incremental cost, which involves multiplying each unit by the marginal cost of that unit, *id.* at H-3. This method, however, does not appear to be used for the attributable cost calculation.

driver" used to calculate the cost elasticity. For example, the Postal Service uses the number of stops as the cost driver for city carrier access.[20] The Postal Service suggests that such a measure is preferable to similar fully distributed cost methods using mail volume. An arbitrary choice of the cost driver, however, can significantly affect cost estimates. Those effects, in turn, would entail variation in the cost estimates used as a basis for Ramsey pricing, or any other regulated pricing methods for that matter.

A second approach that the Postal Service uses to calculate the attributable cost of a product is the "constructed marginal cost measure." The Postal Service calculates the effect of a cost driver on cost, and the effect of mail volume on the cost driver, to obtain the marginal cost of mail delivery in terms of mail volume.[21] Again, the accuracy of those estimates will affect the results of Ramsey pricing calculations.

It is sometimes difficult to verify independently whether the cost drivers selected by the Postal Service provide an accurate measure of the economic activities of the enterprise. The ability to evaluate the economic costs and returns from the Postal Service's activities is not only important for regulatory purposes. The Postal Service needs to have economically accurate information about its products and services to manage its own operations, determine the economic viability of its services, and prevent cross-subsidization. Accurate internal business information is necessary to make efficient investment decisions and to reduce or avoid economic losses.

Institutional Costs of the Postal Service

The Postal Service counts about $16 billion (or about 35 per-

---

20. *Id.* at H-6.
21. *Id.* at H-7.

cent) of its total costs as institutional costs.[22] In other words, the Postal Service believes that it cannot attribute more than a third of its costs to any specific service. So a large share of institutional costs appears open to question on the basis of a cursory observation of Postal Service activities. Unlike the joint and common costs of facilities used to produce joint products, as in the case of a local telephone exchange network or an electric power transmission grid, most postal costs are labor costs; it should be possible in the case of the Postal Service to attribute labor costs to distinct activities. In 1994, however, compensation and employee benefits amounted to $39.6 billion, or over 82 percent of the total expenditures of $48.46 billion.[23] It is evident that some proportion of the remaining 18 percent of expenditures—such as sortation equipment—is dedicated to certain classes of service. For example, as mentioned earlier, until 1979, the Postal Service treated advertising expenditures for express mail as nonattributable institutional costs. This suggests that the proportion of institutional costs are exaggerated and do not accurately describe the activities of the Postal Service.

The Postal Service's accounting methodology classifies losses in any given year as institutional costs in future years. Those losses are simply a portion of accounting costs not covered by revenues. Thus, some attributable costs from any year in which a loss occurs are reclassified as institutional costs and are improperly regarded as nonattributable. Costs are attributable or not, regardless of the year in which they are incurred and independent of whether a firm incurs a loss. Such reassignment of costs can only lead to economically ineffectual decision making.

Amid significant controversy, the "estimates" of

---

22. GENERAL ACCOUNTING OFFICE, U.S. POSTAL PRICING: PRICING POSTAL SERVICES IN A COMPETITIVE ENVIRONMENT 7 (1992) [hereinafter GAO REPORT].

23. U.S. POSTAL SERV., 1994 ANNUAL REP. 38 (1994).

nonattributable costs have decreased somewhat since reorganization in 1970. In the 1972, 1975, and 1976 postal rate hearings, the Postal Service used a short-run cost attribution system that included in institutional costs

> all cost for the purchase and lease of buildings, the purchase of equipment and vehicles, expenses for vehicle drivers, vehicle maintenance, building and equipment maintenance and custodial cost, the cost of a mailman's driving or walking his route to deliver mail, one-third of purchased transportation, most supplies including gasoline and oil, and a considerable portion of clerk's time (including window service).[24]

That approach left slightly more than *half* of Postal Service costs unattributed with allocation subject to Postal Service discretion.[25] By the 1994 rate case, the Postal Rate Commission estimated institutional costs to be 34.91 percent, while the Postal Service estimated them to be 36.75 percent.[26]

The exaggeration of the proportion of institutional costs also leads to incorrect conclusions about the Postal Service's production technology. Those costs appear to be fixed costs—that is, they are presumably not volume-sensitive. Therefore, if institutional costs do not depend on volume, an increase in mail volume reduces unit costs and appears to

---

24. Action of the Governors Under 39 U.S.C., Section 3625, and Supporting Record in the Matter of Postal Rate and Fee Increases, Initial Decision, Dkt. No. R74-1, vol. 1, at 3 (Postal Rate Commission 1974), *quoted in* JOHN T. TIERNEY, THE U.S. POSTAL SERVICE: STATUS AND PROSPECTS OF A PUBLIC ENTERPRISE 157 (Auburn House 1988).

25. TIERNEY, *supra* note 24, at 157.

26. Postal Rate and Fee Changes, 1994, Appendices to Opinion and Recommended Decision, Dkt. No. R94-1, vol. 2, App. D (Comparison of Costs Attributed by Cost Segment and Component) at 4 (Postal Rate Commission 1994).

imply the presence of economies of scale. In turn, economies of scale are used as a sufficient condition for natural monopoly. Therefore, a high proportion of institutional costs can be used—incorrectly—to buttress continuation of regulatory barriers to entry to protect the statutory monopoly in first class mail on the ground that the Postal Service is a natural monopoly.

In addition, since the institutional costs are represented as joint and common for all postal services, the presence of those costs incorrectly implies that substantial economies of scope are present. Thus, a high proportion of institutional costs can be used to justify expansion of Postal Service activities in other markets—such as parcel post and express mail—in the name of exploiting economies of scope. For example, the GAO states in its 1992 report that, in comparison with the natural monopoly technology, "[t]he question of whether the Postal Service exhibits 'economies of scope' seems less open to doubt."[27] In short, to recognize that many of the institutional costs are attributable is to refute the "cost-efficiency" justification for the statutory monopoly over first class mail and the Postal Service's expansion into new lines of business.

Another important consequence of high institutional costs, whether or not they are overestimated, is that the relative prices in the Postal Service rate structure are very sensitive to cost allocation schemes, for a high proportion of total costs are shifted around. Moreover, inefficiencies in Postal Service operations that inflate overhead costs increase the impact of cost allocation schemes on prices. Because the Postal Service is not a profit-maximizing enterprise, one cannot expect that its managers keep overhead costs to the level that

---

27. GAO REPORT, *supra* note 22, at 60 (citing Melvyn A. Fuss, *Cost Allocation: How Can the Costs of Postal Services Be Determined?*, in PERSPECTIVES ON POSTAL SERVICE ISSUES 30 (Roger Sherman ed., AEI Press 1980)).

would be observed for private companies carrying out similar tasks, nor would one expect that the relative proportions of institutional and attributable costs correspond to efficient levels.

The Difficulty of Preventing Cross-Subsidization by the Postal Service

The Postal Service is concerned that its prices are not competitive with parcel post and express mail. Postmaster General Runyon stresses the need for "price flexibility" as a means of responding to competitive pressures.[28] Essentially, price flexibility of this type requires a shifting of institutional costs away from markets in which the Postal Service faces competition and toward markets where it holds a statutory monopoly. Given the high likelihood of incorrect measurement of institutional costs and cost inefficiencies, such cost shifting can easily lead to cross-subsidization of competitive activities by the Postal Service's captive customers.

There are few safeguards against such cross-subsidization. As we have already observed, the Postal Service can carry out a cross-subsidization program by following standard cost allocation rules if it can inflate the proportion of institutional costs. Moreover, since the Postal Service already has a presence in the competitive markets for parcel post and express mail, it is difficult for regulators to distinguish incremental costs devoted to those activities from growth in institutional costs.

Market safeguards against cross-subsidization also are absent because of the Postal Service's statutory monopoly. Competitive firms generally cannot cross-subsidize because cross-subsidizing induces competitive entry. If a service of-

---

28. Address by Postmaster General Marvin Runyon to the National Press Club, Washington, D.C. (Jan. 31, 1995) (available in LEXIS News Library) [hereinafter *National Press Club Speech*].

fered by a firm is contributing greater revenues than its standalone cost, and if entry barriers are not excessive, then competitors will enter the market and profitably supply that service. If the markets providing subsidies are protected by statutory entry barriers, however, such competition cannot occur. The statutory monopoly over first class mail delivery makes it relatively easy for the Postal Service to engage in cross-subsidization of competitive activities (such as parcel post and overnight mail) and to pass the cost along to captive customers.

A profit-maximizing firm generally does not have an incentive to cross-subsidize. The Postal Service's behavior, however, suggests that it maximizes volume, which rises as the Postal Service expands into new services or reduces its prices relative to those of its competitors. Indeed, the Postal Service has shown a willingness to suffer significant losses while maintaining or increasing volume, or while entering into or remaining in markets that private, competitive firms have proven can be profitably served without government intervention. Such behavior by the Postal Service is not consistent with profit-maximizing behavior (or, for that matter, its statutory mandate) but is consistent with the objective of maximizing volume and employment.

Litigation over Inverse Elasticity Pricing

The Post Office's ratemaking procedures repeatedly produced cross-subsidies running from first class mail to other mail services. In reaction to that practice, Congress in 1970 constrained the discretion of postal managers in setting rates for the classes of mail.[29] Through the Postal Reorganization Act of 1970, Congress established the Postal Rate Commission to

---

29. William Ty Mayton, *The Mission and Methods of the Postal Service*, in GOVERNING THE POSTAL SERVICE, *supra* note 2, at 60, 102.

recommend rates for classes of mail on the basis of the guidelines delineated in section 3622(b) of the act.[30] The guidelines were ambiguous, however, and the Postal Service continued to apportion costs in ratemaking as it had before by using inverse elasticity pricing techniques.[31]

In 1976 the Postal Service was taken to task for its ratemaking procedures by the U.S. Court of Appeals for the District of Columbia Circuit in *National Association of Greeting Card Publishers v. United States Postal Service*.[32] After examining the legislative intent, the court observed:

> Discrimination in postal ratemaking in favor of certain preferred classes of mail and to the great disadvantage of first class mail has long been a part of our postal system . . . . In seeking postal reform through the 1970 Act it was a central and express aim of both Houses of Congress to end the abuses of this practice.[33]

On that basis, the court rejected the Postal Service's use of the inverse elasticity rule and agreed with the argument that the rule "preserved historical rate differentials and otherwise unduly and unreasonably discriminated against first class mail."[34]

In rejecting the Postal Service's use of the inverse elasticity rule, the D.C. Circuit turned instead to the nine factors listed in section 3622(b) to be used in setting postal

---

30. 39 U.S.C. § 3622(b).
31. Mayton, *supra* note 29, at 101-02.
32. 569 F.2d 570 (D.C. Cir. 1976) [hereinafter *National Ass'n of Greeting Card Publishers I*].
33. *Id.* at 587-88.
34. *Id.* at 584.

rates.[35] The overriding criterion by which Congress intended the Postal Rate Commission to calculate postal rates, the court ruled, was section 3622(b)(3), which states: "the requirement that each class of mail or type of mail service bear the direct and indirect postal costs attributable to that class or type plus that portion of all other costs of the Postal Service reasonably assignable to such class or type."[36] The court concluded that "the very words of subsection (b)(3) disclose its concern that each class of mail and postal service shoulder all the postal costs that may reasonably be traced to the provision of that class or service."[37] Section 3622(b)(3) thus required the Postal Service to use a cost-of-service rather than a value-of-service methodology to allocate costs. Only by attributing costs in this way, the D.C. Circuit reasoned, would postal rates be set in the fair and equitable manner that Congress intended.[38]

In 1978, in response to litigation over the failure of the Postal Service and the Postal Rate Commission to conform to its 1976 decision, the D.C. Circuit reaffirmed that decision and underscored the requirement that costs, both direct and indirect, be allocated to the maximum degree possible to the class of mail that incurs them.[39] The decision rejected the Postal Service's continuing efforts to allocate more than half of its costs to first class mail through the use of the inverse elasticity rule.

In 1983, however, after disgruntled second class mailers shifted their litigation to the Second Circuit in a successful effort to elude the D.C. Circuit's ruling, the Supreme Court granted certiorari to resolve the resulting split between the circuit courts. In its opinion the Supreme Court rejected the

---

35. 39 U.S.C. § 3622(b).
36. *Id.* § 3622(b)(3).
37. *National Ass'n of Greeting Card Publishers I,* 569 F.2d at 585.
38. *Id.* at 585–86.
39. National Ass'n of Greeting Card Publishers *v.* United States Postal Serv., 607 F.2d 392 (D.C. Cir. 1978).

Second Circuit's embrace of a short-run costing approach but also rebuffed the D.C. Circuit's continuing efforts to subject postal ratemaking to strict statutory controls.[40] Instead, the Court deferred to the Postal Rate Commission's methods of setting rates and its argument that section 3622(b) did not mandate any particular method for allocating costs.[41] The Court reiterated the familiar principle that administrative agencies should have broad discretion to interpret the statutes concerning their powers, and it reasoned that such judicial deference to agency interpretations of law would effect Congress's intent that discretionary matters be left to the expertise of objective agency officials.[42]

Such discretion, of course, does not give the Postal Rate Commission so much latitude as to employ a distorted version of the inverse elasticity rule that rests on a misinterpretation of the theory of Ramsey pricing—which, as we shall demonstrate presently, is the fatal flaw in the 1992 GAO report that the Postal Service in 1995 recommended to the Postal Rate Commission as a guide to future ratemaking.

Remedies for Cost Misallocation by the Postal Service

Three principal remedies would prevent the Postal Service from misallocating cost. The first would be to open all postal markets to competition. Such a policy would eliminate cross-subsidies in the rate structure of the Postal Service and would wring out any of its economic inefficiencies because both of those conditions would create profitable opportunities for firms to enter the market and offer lower prices.

A second remedy, not mutually inconsistent with the

---

40. National Ass'n of Greeting Card Publishers v. United States Postal Serv., 462 U.S. 810 (1983).
41. *Id.* at 834.
42. *Id.* at 822.

first, would be to break up the Postal Service along product lines to avoid any incorrect identification of attributable costs as being joint and common.

A third remedy would be an alternative to the first two: remove the Postal Service from all markets but those in which it has a statutory monopoly so as to avoid the possibility of subsidies' going from protected to competitive activities.

We discuss the first and third alternatives in more detail in our policy recommendations in chapter 7.

MISUSE OF RAMSEY PRICING PRINCIPLES

A misuse of Ramsey pricing principles underlies the GAO's recommendation that Congress grant the Postal Service the freedom to price according to the inverse elasticity rule. The same deficiency implicitly underlies Postmaster General Runyon's call for greater pricing flexibility. We begin by reviewing the concept of Ramsey pricing and then show where errors of economic reasoning arise in the arguments of the GAO and the postmaster general.

Ramsey Pricing

Ramsey pricing is a method of allocating fixed costs and joint and common costs for a regulated firm or public enterprise. If it were feasible financially, economic welfare would be maximized by setting the price of each product equal to its marginal (or incremental) cost. If there are economies of scale, however, marginal cost pricing yields insufficient revenues to cover the firm's total cost. Prices must therefore exceed marginal cost for the firm to recover fixed costs and joint and common costs and thus continue to supply the goods in question.

But every deviation of price from marginal cost creates some inefficiency—first, because it provides an incentive for consumers to switch to those goods whose prices are raised only modestly relative to their true marginal cost, and second, because every rise in price restricts demand by cutting into consumer purchasing power. Ramsey pricing denotes those second-best prices that are Pareto optimal, subject to the requirement that they yield revenues sufficient to cover the total costs incurred by the supplier of the products in question. The damage to welfare is minimized if the firm can cover its revenue shortfall through smaller increases in the prices of the goods whose demands are elastic and through larger increases in the prices of goods whose demands are comparatively inelastic.[43]

Firms usually obtain Ramsey prices by maximizing the sum of consumer surplus and producer surplus subject to the constraint that the revenues the firm generates cover its costs. The standard approach to deriving Ramsey prices is itself subject to theoretical dispute, however, because it ignores effects on the distribution of income and assumes that the income effects of price changes are insignificant.[44] Derivations of Ramsey prices often assume that a change in the price of one of the firm's products will not affect the demand for its other products.[45] We review the derivation of Ramsey prices

---

43. *See* Frank P. Ramsey, *A Contribution to the Theory of Taxation*, 37 ECON. J. 47 (1927). For a review of the subsequent literature, see William J. Baumol, *Ramsey Pricing*, in 4 THE NEW PALGRAVE: A DICTIONARY OF ECONOMICS 49–51 (John Eatwell, Murray Milgate & Peter Newman eds., MacMillan Press Limited 1987); William J. Baumol & David F. Bradford, *Optimal Departures from Marginal Cost Pricing*, 60 AM. ECON. REV. 265 (1970).

44. *See* SPULBER, *supra* note 7, at 166–68; Martin S. Feldstein, *Distributional Equity and the Optimal Structure of Public Prices*, 62 AM. ECON. REV. 32 (1972); Martin S. Feldstein, *Equity and Efficiency in Public Sector Pricing: The Optimal Two-Part Tariff*, 86 Q.J. ECON. 175 (1972).

45. The analysis of Frank A. Scott, Jr., *Assessing USA Postal Ratemaking: An Application of Ramsey Prices*, 34 J. INDUS. ECON. 279 (1986), and Roger Sherman & Anthony George, *Second-Best Pricing for the U.S. Postal Service*, 45 S. ECON. J. 685 (1979), account for cross-elasticities of demand and income effects. Analyses that assume zero cross-price elastici-

in the appendix to this chapter.

Moreover, if the firm incorrectly characterizes attributable costs as joint costs (or vice versa), it will bias the Ramsey prices and preclude the welfare-maximizing result, as the appendix to this chapter demonstrates analytically. As we noted earlier, the apparent need to allocate institutional costs by using demand factors grows in importance the more the Postal Service is able, through questionable accounting practices, to count attributable costs as overhead. If instead such costs were correctly attributed to specific activities of the Postal Service, many problems of cost allocation would disappear.

The Error Underlying the GAO's Recommendation That the Postal Service Employ the Inverse Elasticity Rule

The GAO's recommendation that the Postal Service use the inverse elasticity rule is theoretically flawed because the GAO would have the Postal Service use estimates of the price elasticity of demand for first class mail that are predicated on regulatory barriers to entry into postal markets. According to the GAO, "[t]he Postal Service believes that demand factors should play a major role in overhead cost allocation, whereas the Commission places less weight on demand factors in its pricing decisions than the Postal Service does."[46] In its report to Congress, the GAO recommends the following:

---

ties of demand include O. A. Davis & A. B. Whinston, *Welfare Economics and the Theory of Second Best,* 32 REV. ECON. STUD. 1 (1965); Baumol & Bradford, *supra* note 43; Abba P. Lerner, *On Optimal Taxes with an Untaxable Sector,* 60 AM. ECON. REV. 284 (1970). *See also* Leonard Waverman, *Pricing Principles: How Should Postal Rates Be Set?, in* PERSPECTIVES ON POSTAL RATES 7 (Roger Sherman ed., AEI Press 1980).

46. GAO REPORT, *supra* note 22, at 4.

> [T]o give the Postal Service more competitive flexibility, GAO believes Congress should reexamine the nine ratemaking criteria set forth in the Postal Reorganization Act and consider amending them to state that (1) in allocating institutional costs, demand factors—including elasticities of demand—are to be given a weight that takes into account the need to maintain the long-term viability of the Postal Service as a nationwide full-service provider of postal services and that (2) such use of demand factors will not be inconsistent with the rate criterion requiring the establishment of a fair and equitable rate schedule as long as each mail class recovers the direct and indirect costs attributable to that service and makes some contribution to institutional costs. Congress should also consider reexamining the provisions of section 403(c) of the Postal Reorganization Act to determine if volume discounting by the Postal Service would in fact result in "undue or unreasonable discrimination" among mailer and "undue or unreasonable preference" to a mailer.[47]

Even if a legitimate need for overhead cost allocation exists, the GAO has applied demand-based pricing rules with deceptive oversimplification to the operations of the Postal Service.

The demand for a firm's good is always more price elastic than the total market demand for that good—unless the firm is a monopolist protected by entry barriers, in which case the price elasticities of demand for the firm and the market closely correspond. Generally, the firm faces a demand function that reflects the reactions of competitors and potential en-

---

47. *Id.* at 8–9.

trants, which increase price elasticity.[48]

The application of demand-based pricing yields the familiar inverse elasticity rule for all services:

$$(P_i - MC_i)/P_i = K/\eta_i,$$

where $i = 1, 2, 3, 4, 5$ is an index representing the five classes of postal services. The other terms are defined as follows:

P_i = price of service i,
MC_i = marginal (attributable) cost of service i,
K = a constant reflecting the shadow price of the break-even constraint,
η_i = the price elasticity of demand for service i.

The ratio of relative markups for any two services is governed therefore by the inverse ratio of elasticities of those two services, for any two services i and j:

$$\frac{\frac{(P_i - MC_i)}{P_i}}{\frac{(P_j - MC_j)}{P_j}} = \frac{\eta_j}{\eta_i}.$$

The elasticity of demand is defined as the percentage change in quantity demanded divided by the percentage change in price. Let $D_i(P_i)$ represent the demand function for service i, which depends on the price of service i. Then, the elasticity of

---

48. *See* William E. Landes & Richard A. Posner, *Market Power in Antitrust Cases,* 94 HARV. L. REV. 937, 945 (1981).

demand is defined by:

$$\eta_i = \frac{dD_i(P_i)}{dP_i} \frac{P_i}{D_i(P_i)}, \quad i = 1, 2, 3, 4, 5.$$

The elasticity of demand is negative because a price increase lowers the quantity demanded.

The current approach to calculating elasticities of demand for postal services is based on estimates of the effect of a percentage change in postal rates on the percentage change in postal volume for a given class of mail. Professor George S. Tolley of the University of Chicago, whose testimony the Postal Rate Commission has relied upon in ratemaking proceedings, had used that method to estimate that the long-run elasticity of demand for first class mail is $-.188$.[49] This general type of estimation provides a reasonably accurate description of the elasticity of the Postal Service's demand, although it has engendered some disagreement about the econometric methodology used.[50]

The larger problem with the GAO's approach is that its estimates of the price elasticities of demand for the various classes of mail are contingent on the statutory barrier to entry that the Postal Service enjoys with respect to first class mail. The price elasticity for first class mail is consequently lower than it would be if there were no statutory monopoly. Professor William J. Baumol and one of the present authors have written about this same problem in telecommunications regulation:

> Application of Ramsey analysis to regulation is subject to [an] important caveat because feasi-

---

49. Direct Testimony of George S. Tolley on Behalf of the United States Postal Service, Postal Rate and Fee Changes, 1994, Dkt. No. R94-1 (Postal Rate Commission 1994).

50. GAO REPORT, *supra* note 22, at 74-78.

bility of the calculations is likely to require them to take the pertinent demand elasticities as a given. In the language of economics, these elasticities are then treated as exogenous. But regulators considerably influence the firm's demand elasticity by their decisions and policies that affect the firm's actual or potential competitors. Clearly, severe constraint of firms' entry and pricing will somewhat immunize each enterprise from the competitive pressures of others. That immunity from competition will reduce the elasticity of each supplier's demand—that is, it will reduce the loss of business that results from a rise in its prices. The firm's price elasticity of demand thus must be said to be endogenously determined by the regulatory process itself. With such regulatorily influenced demand elasticities, it is not clear that Ramsey prices calculated *ex ante* will be those necessary for economic efficiency.[51]

When one applies this same reasoning to the Postal Service, it is clear that demand-based pricing simply reflects the statutory monopoly over first class mail and thus conveys little information about either consumers' willingness to pay for postal services or the opportunity costs of alternative suppliers. Those elasticity estimates have precision without rigor.

This fallacy in postal ratemaking has not escaped notice in the past. Leonard Waverman wrote in 1980 that the inverse elasticity rule "does not contemplate a firm that has one monopoly service and competes with other firms in its other services."[52] He observed that the true elasticity of de-

---

51. BAUMOL & SIDAK, *supra* note 8, at 40–41 (footnote omitted).
52. Waverman, *supra* note 45, at 20.

mand for first class mail would result in its being assigned a much lower share of institutional costs:

> The Postal Rate Commission has not dropped the inverse elasticity rule. Utilizing the words "competition" or "value of service," the commission sets rates above attributable costs in the same fashion as in the past: first-class mail bears the great percentage of institutional costs. Yet it is clearly first-class mail that faces the greatest potential competition. Electronic funds transfer may, within the decade, substantially lessen the number of first-class pieces carried by the Postal Service. The loss of traffic will destroy the elaborate house of cards on which the Postal Service and the commission have erected their rate structure. Without first-class mail to carry most of the common costs, rates will have to be increased for the other categories of mail.[53]

The Department of Justice similarly observed in 1977:

> First class mail users have the most inelastic demand; by eliminating competitive options through enforcement of the express statutes, this inelasticity of demand is maintained. Therefore, the lion's share of common costs is assigned to first class.[54]

Still other economists in the 1980s debated in the academic

---

53. *Id.* at 24.
54. U.S. DEPARTMENT OF JUSTICE, CHANGING THE PRIVATE EXPRESS LAWS: COMPETITIVE ALTERNATIVES AND THE U.S. POSTAL SERVICE 12 (1977).

literature the extent to which, given these "cooked up" elasticities, demand-based pricing rules are an unreliable way to determine the most efficient means of allocating joint and common costs across postal customers.[55]

The GAO also recognizes this problem, for it states that it has "assumed that First-Class Mail is the most inelastic class because it has stronger monopoly restrictions than the other classes of mail."[56] Nonetheless, the GAO asserts—erroneously—that "the fact that elasticities may differ for different classes of mail because the law allows for different amounts of competition in those classes does not negate the validity of [the inverse elasticity rule] for ratemaking in the Postal Service."[57] Instead, the GAO argues that those elasticities should simply be taken as a given for pricing purposes "[g]iven the market structure within which the Postal Service must operate."[58] The GAO makes that assertion despite its observation that the econometric estimates of demand elasticities omit a number of factors:

> The omitted variables might include private competitors' price, the quality of Postal Service products and services relative to those of its

---

55. William B. Tye, *The Postal Service: Economics Made Simplistic*, 3 J. POL'Y ANALYSIS & MGMT. 62 (1983); Frank A. Scott, Jr., *The Pricing Policy of the Postal Service: Economics Misapplied*, 4 J. POL'Y ANALYSIS & MGMT. 251 (1985); William B. Tye, *The Pricing Policy of the Postal Service: Policymaking Misunderstood*, 4 J. POL'Y ANALYSIS & MGMT. 256 (1985).

56. GAO REPORT, *supra* note 22, at 66. *See also id.* at 30-31 ("Because of historical experience and First-Class Mail protection from unrestricted competition by the Private Express Statutes, postal ratemaking experts believe that this service has a relatively inelastic demand—i.e., the demand for the service is not greatly affected by changes in postal rates."); *id.* at 64 ("[T]he relative inelasticity of First-Class Mail may be largely due to the legal monopoly granted to the Postal Service.").

57. *Id.*

58. *Id.*

competitors' entrepreneurship, product and marketing innovations (advances in computers and telecommunications), and exogenous changes in market conditions and in consumers' tastes and needs.[59]

Even if additional variables were included, as the GAO implies that they should be, the estimation of demand elasticities still would fail to give an accurate representation of competitor responses in the absence of the regulatory barriers to entry enjoyed by the Postal Service.

The Correct Demand Elasticity for Computing Ramsey Prices for the Postal Service

When we correctly assume that the artificially induced firm price elasticity of demand for the Postal Service does *not* equal the actual market price elasticity of demand, we can immediately see the fallacy of the GAO's analysis concerning the suitability of the inverse elasticity rule. To illustrate this point, suppose that entry were permitted into first class mail and that the new entrants' actions could be described by a supply function $S(P_1)$ that depended on the Postal Service's price for the service, P_1. Then the Postal Service's residual demand for the service would equal the difference between the market demand $D(P_1)$ and the supply response of competitive firms:

$$D_1(P_1) = D(P_1) - S(P_1).$$

Therefore, the price elasticity of demand for the Postal Service for first class mail η_1 can be expressed in terms of the entire market's price elasticity of demand η, the Postal Service's market share s, and the (positive) price elasticity of

---

59. *Id.* at 74.

supply of the other firms on the competitive fringe of the market η^s.[60] That is,

$$\eta_1 = \frac{\eta}{s} - \frac{\eta^s(1-s)}{s}.$$

By statute, s must equal one because the supply of competing firms is held at zero. In general, competition affects the elasticity of the firm's demand in a more complicated manner—that is, it cannot simply be subtracted. A complete analysis would need to take into account the costs of entry and operation for competitors. In any case, competition will increase the Postal Service's elasticity of demand, as it has clearly done in parcel post and express mail.

In other words, the Private Express Statutes require that the Postal Service have *all* the market for the delivery of first class mail. That requirement causes the second term in the numerator to become zero—which prematurely ends any inquiry by the GAO into the extent to which a fringe of competing suppliers would enter the delivery of first class mail *if allowed to do so*. The price elasticity of demand for first class mail is artificially low because the Private Express Statutes forbid competition and thus arbitrarily drive down to zero the price elasticity of fringe supply (which affects the relevant price elasticity of demand). The low elasticity of demand that the GAO asserts to exist for first class mail is then seen to be a regulatory contrivance—one preordained by the Postal Service's historical resistance to allowing competitive entry into first class mail through relaxation or repeal of the Private Express Statutes.

Another way to understand the elasticity of demand for first class mail is to consider the effects of having a substitute

---

60. The elasticity of supply is $\eta^s = (dS(P_1)/dP_1)(P_1/S(P_1))$, which is positive because the supply function is increasing in the price. The market share of the Postal Service is $s = D_1(P_1)/D(P_1)$.

service. The products of the Postal Service are differentiated from those of private carriers in terms of brand name, pickup locations, service quality, and other features. Suppose that there is a competitive substitute for first class mail. Let $D(P_1, P_S)$ represent the demand for the Postal Service's first class mail, evaluated at the price of first class service, P_1 and the price of the competitive substitute, P_S. The own-price elasticity of demand for first class mail is

$$\eta_1(P_1,P_S) = \frac{\partial D(P_1,P_S)}{\partial P_1} \frac{P_1}{D(P_1,P_S)}.$$

The entry barriers established by the Private Express Statutes can be modeled as a very high price for the competitive substitute. Under reasonable conditions, a higher price for the substitute will lower the elasticity of demand for first class mail.[61] Therefore, legal and regulatory restrictions on substitutes for first class mail have the effect of artificially reducing the elasticity of demand for first class mail.

Although the GAO report acknowledges that the statutory monopoly over the delivery of first class mail lowers the price elasticity of demand for such mail,[62] the GAO nonetheless fails to recognize that this critical fact invalidates the reasoning by which the GAO reaches its conclusion that the

---

61. The effect of the price of the substitute on the elasticity of demand is

$\partial \eta(P_1,P_S)/\partial P_S = [P_1/(D(P_1,P_S))^2] \times$
$\qquad [D(P_1,P_S)D_{12}(P_1,P_S) - D_1(P_1,P_S)D_2(P_1,P_S)].$

Because the two products are substitutes, a higher price for the substitute would increase demand for first class mail, $D_2(P_1,P_S) > 0$. If the cross-price effect is either positive or not too small, $D_{12}(P_1,P_S) \geq [D_1(P_1,P_S)D_2(P_1,P_S)/D(P_1, P_S)]$, then the demand for first class mail becomes less elastic as the price of the substitute rises.

62. GAO REPORT, *supra* note 22, at 62–63.

inverse elasticity rule should govern the allocation of institutional costs to the various classes of mail. We have no reason to suppose (as the GAO evidently does) that pricing according to the inverse elasticity rule would maximize consumer welfare when the Postal Service's price elasticity of demand for first class mail is an artifact of legal barriers to entry.

A. Michael Spence, a respected economist who is the current dean of Stanford Business School, argued in 1983 that the distorting effect of the Private Express Statutes on the price elasticity of demand for first class mail does not by itself imply that first class rates derived from the inverse elasticity rule are excessive:

> It is certainly true that if the private express statutes were dropped, the elasticity of demand for USPS services would rise in first class mail, and that would tend to reduce those rates as they emerge from optimal pricing formulas. But the conclusion that the first class mail rates were artificially high does not follow. The *issue* is whether it is a good thing or not to expose USPS to competition. That issue is not decided by describing correctly one of the consequences of allowing competition. Therefore, without prejudging the whole issue, to repeal the private express statutes on the ground that they artificially create a demand facing the Postal Service for first class mail that is inelastic, would be to do it for the wrong, or at least an insufficient reason.[63]

---

63. A. Michael Spence, *Regulating the Structural Environment of the Postal Service, in* THE FUTURE OF THE POSTAL SERVICE, 197, 206–07 (Joel L. Fleishman ed., Aspen Institute & Praeger Publishers 1983) (emphasis in original).

Spence raises a valid point, but it is not one that detracts from our conclusion that the GAO's proposal for inverse elasticity pricing by the Postal Service is analytically flawed.

As we showed in chapter 3, one cannot credibly conclude that the Postal Service is a natural monopoly. Competition is therefore an available option should we conclude, in response to the question that Spence poses, that it is desirable to expose the Postal Service to competition. The analysis in chapter 4 in turn showed that a poorly regulated postal monopoly has no advantage over competition in the provision of postal services. In short, the Private Express Statutes directly harm consumer welfare, and the alternative of competition is readily available. We should not be taken to say that repeal of the Private Express Statutes is justified simply because they have the secondary effect of distorting Ramsey pricing principles when applied to the Postal Service in the simplistic manner advocated by the GAO. In short, our analysis provides a sufficient reason not only to reject the recommendations of the GAO's 1992 report, but also to repeal the Private Express Statutes.

The Postal Service's Pursuit of "Profit"

Since regulators first addressed Ramsey pricing in ratemaking proceedings several decades ago, the concept has invited the recurrent but uninformed criticism that it is tantamount to a rule allowing the supposedly regulated monopolist to charge whatever the traffic will bear.[64] That criticism is incorrect because it ignores that Ramsey prices are constrained to yield profits no higher than the competitive earnings level, while the profits of a price-discriminating monopolist are uncon-

---

64. *See* BAUMOL & SIDAK, *supra* note 8, at 52-53 & n.2 (citing American Tel. & Tel. Co., Dkt. No. 19129, 64 F.C.C.2d 131, 469-70 ¶¶ 1121-24 (1976)).

strained. Prices that are set subject to a profit constraint will be considerably lower than those adopted in the absence of such a constraint.[65]

The irony of the GAO's 1992 report on postal pricing, and of the postmaster general's 1995 call for greater pricing flexibility, is that they are in essence recommendations for the Postal Service to approximate not Ramsey pricing but rather unconstrained price discrimination by a firm having a guaranteed monopoly in one market and facing competition in its other markets. The Postal Service has demonstrated a proclivity to characterize, through incorrect measurement or misallocation, an inordinate share of its total costs as institutional costs. The GAO would then place a greater share of those inflated institutional costs on customers of first class mail—based on the GAO's specious interpretation of the inverse elasticity rule, which fails to adjust for the fact that the price elasticity of demand for first class mail is artificially low because the statutory monopoly on the delivery of first class mail excludes any possibility of competitive entry.

In short, the economic essence of what the GAO and the postmaster general advocate is that the Postal Service should be allowed to charge first class customers whatever the traffic will bear and charge other customers of other classes of mail prices that undercut private competitors. Thus, unrestricted pricing combined with statutory monopoly will yield monopoly profits for the Postal Service. Expansion into competitive markets will yield additional profits if there are economies of scope between the provision of first and third class mail and the provision of expanded services such as parcel post and express mail. If such expansion is subsidized, however, the expansion creates economic inefficiencies. Such a set of outcomes would comport with the postmaster general's prediction that, if the Postal Service were granted greater pricing

---

65. *Id.*

flexibility and freedom to enter new markets, the enterprise "could become a profit center for the federal government."[66]

In what sense will the Postal Service earn such "profits"? The Postal Service typically runs losses that accrue as institutional costs to be recovered in the future through postal revenues.[67] In May 1995 the postmaster general stated in a speech, "We are going to pay down billions of dollars in prior year deficits and debt, and put the Postal Service on solid financial footing."[68] That recovery of prior years' losses represents another way in which attributable costs are mischaracterized as institutional costs: some portion of last year's unrecovered attributable costs return in the current year as *institutional* costs because of the Postal Service's determination to recover prior years' losses. If the Postal Service earns revenues in excess of costs, those returns will presumably accumulate as a surplus. As we noted previously, the Postal Service pays no dividends. Continuation of cost-of-service postal ratemaking means that positive net earnings at best will serve to delay rate increases. The Postal Service has an incentive to absorb this "free cash flow" by increasing expenditures or investing in future expansion of postal services.[69]

Unlike privately owned companies, the Postal Service has no market test for those investment decisions. Competitive firms must take into account the cost of capital in their investment decisions. The Postal Service is relatively immune from

---

66. *National Press Club Speech, supra* note 28.

67. Postal Rate and Fee Changes, 1994, Opinion and Recommended Decision, Dkt. No. R94-1, vol. 1, at II-16 to II-24 (Postal Rate Commission 1994).

68. Address by Postmaster General Marvin Runyon to the National Postal Forum, Nashville, Tennessee 2 (May 8, 1995).

69. *See* Michael C. Jensen, *Agency Costs of Free Cash Flow, Corporate Finance, and Takeovers*, 76 AM. ECON. REV. PAPERS & PROC. 323 (1986); *see also* PAUL MILGROM & JOHN ROBERTS, ECONOMICS, ORGANIZATION AND MANAGEMENT 492–94 (Prentice Hall 1992).

such considerations. Were it not for the fact that the Postal Service is *losing* money, it would be difficult for those reasons to evaluate the extent to which it was generating profits. Moreover, the Postal Service's reporting requirements differ substantially from those of publicly traded companies. Since the Postal Service employs accounting methods that diverge from those used by private firms and is highly secretive about its costs, it would be difficult to compare its profits with the accounting profits of private companies.

Conclusion

The postal ratemaking process has unusual cost allocation and accounting procedures that bear little relationship to economic theory. Conventional regulatory safeguards to prevent cost misallocation are absent from postal rate regulation. The statutory monopoly over letter mail conferred on the Postal Service by the Private Express Statutes intentionally suppresses competition and consumer choice. The Postal Service's understanding of Ramsey pricing principles is faulty.

When those factors are combined in the postal ratemaking process, it becomes clear that reliance on inverse elasticity pricing could maximize consumer welfare only by sheer accident. It is far more likely that postal rates set in such a manner would harm consumer welfare and competitive markets for postal services. It would be a mistake to employ inverse elasticity pricing until postal regulation has been dramatically reformed, or until the Postal Service has been commercialized and the Private Express Statutes have been repealed.

Appendix: Ramsey Pricing and Cost Misallocation

This appendix reviews the basic Ramsey pricing framework without income effects and with independent demands. It examines the consequences of cost misallocation for the standard Ramsey pricing formula.

To illustrate the Ramsey approach, we restrict attention to the case of two goods. Good 1 represents services protected by statutory monopoly, particularly first class mail, and good 2 represents services not subject to restricted entry, such as parcel post or express mail.

The demand functions for the two services are assumed to be independent of the price of the other service, although in practice there are also cross-price effects on the demand for postal services. Let P_1 and P_2 represent postal rates and let $D_1(P_1)$ and $D_2(P_2)$ be the demands for the services. Both the protected service and the competitive service will depend on prices for substitute services offered by the private sector, although we ignore those effects in presenting the Ramsey framework.

We can represent the total cost of the two services by a simple functional form that is sufficient to address the main issues at hand. Let Q_1 and Q_2 be the volume levels for the two services. Total costs are given by

$$C(Q_1, Q_2) = F + C_1(Q_1) + C_2(Q_2). \tag{6.1}$$

The cost functions $C_1(Q_1)$ and $C_2(Q_2)$ represent attributable costs for the two services, and the fixed cost F represents joint and common costs that must be incurred if either one or both of the services are produced. Generally speaking, joint and common costs can depend on the volume levels as well, although for our purpose it is sufficient to consider a fixed level for those costs.

Marginal costs for the two goods are given by $MC_1 = C_1'(Q_1)$ and $MC_2 = C_2'(Q_2)$. The attributable cost functions can include fixed cost components.

The second-best pricing problem addresses the issue of pricing to recover costs for a regulated firm or public enterprise. The pricing methodology is restricted to constant per unit prices, as opposed to two-part or multipart pricing.[70] The term *first-best* prices usually denotes *marginal cost* prices.

In the single-good case, economies of scale mean that the marginal cost is less than average cost,

$$C_i'(Q_i) < \frac{C_i(Q_i)}{Q_i}.$$

This condition implies that a marginal cost price would not recover costs. The second-best price is one that exactly recovers costs and thus equals average cost evaluated at the corresponding demand level. For a single product demand $D_i(P_i)$, that price is given by

$$P_i = \frac{C_i(D_i(P_i))}{D_i(P_i)}, \qquad i = 1, 2.$$

The case of two or more products is only a bit more complicated. Economies of scale are said to exist if the sum of marginal cost times output is less than total cost,

$$C_1'(Q_1)Q_1 + C_2'(Q_2)Q_2 < C(Q_1, Q_2).$$

That condition may be due to economies of scale attributable to either of the two products or to fixed costs that are joint and common. The presence of joint and common costs prevents the definition of "average costs" for either of the two products. The second-best pricing problem consists of selecting welfare-maximizing prices that cover total costs.

With independent demands and in the absence of income effects, consumer surplus for each product is represented by

---

70. For a discussion of second-best two-part tariffs and nonlinear pricing, see SPULBER, *supra* note 7, at 200-38.

$$CS_i(P_i) = \int_{P_i}^{\infty} D_i(P)dP, \qquad i = 1, 2.$$

Producer's surplus is given by

$$\Pi(P_1,P_2) = P_1 D(P_1) + P_2 D(P_2) - C(D_1(P_1), D_2(P_2)). \qquad (6.2)$$

The regulatory objective is to choose prices that maximize total surplus subject to a break-even condition for the producer,

$$\text{Max}_{P_1,P_2} \; CS(P_1) + CS(P_2) + \Pi(P_1,P_2) \qquad (6.3)$$

subject to

$$\Pi(P_1,P_2) \geq 0. \qquad (6.4)$$

Let λ be the Lagrange multiplier associated with the break-even constraint. The first-order conditions for the regulator's problem include the following:

$$(P_i - MC_i)D_1'(P_i) + \lambda[(P_i - MC_i)D_i'(P_i) + D_i(P_i)] = 0, \qquad i = 1, 2. \qquad (6.5)$$

At an interior optimum at which prices are positive, the break-even constraint will be binding if marginal cost pricing fails to cover total cost. Then, the shadow price on the break-even constraint will be positive, $\lambda > 0$.

Rewriting the pricing conditions using the elasticity of demand yields the inverse elasticity rule,

$$\frac{P_i - MC_i}{P_i} = \frac{-\lambda}{1+\lambda} \frac{1}{\eta_i}, \qquad i = 1, 2. \qquad (6.6)$$

The first factor on the right-hand side, $-\lambda/(1+\lambda)$, is the "Ramsey number." It represents the product of the relative markup and the elasticity of demand, $[(P_i-MC_i)/P_i]\eta_i$. The Ramsey prices P_1 and P_2 solve the conditions in equation (6.6) and the break-even equation,

$$\Pi(P_1, P_2) = 0. \tag{6.7}$$

Taking the ratio of relative markups using equation (6.6), we can eliminate the Ramsey number,

$$\frac{(P_1-MC_1)/P_1}{(P_2-MC_2)/P_2} = \frac{1/\eta_1}{1/\eta_2}. \tag{6.8}$$

The Ramsey prices P_1 and P_2 are then obtained by solving two conditions: the break-even condition (6.7) and the relative markup condition (6.8).

Given the preceding analysis, we can calculate the Ramsey prices (using equations (6.7) and (6.8)) without going through the optimization procedure. Of course, applying that method correctly requires accurate measurement of marginal costs and demand elasticities.

What are the consequences of misallocating costs by treating attributable costs as joint and common? To address that question, let some proportion of attributable cost for product 2 be counted as joint and common, $aC_2(Q_2)$. Then joint and common costs, E, are

$$E = F + aC_2(Q_2). \tag{6.9}$$

The allocation of costs in this manner should have no effect on the Ramsey pricing calculations because an increase in output will result in an increase in total cost, regardless of how costs are classified.

Suppose, however, that the regulator fails to recognize the output-sensitive nature of joint and common cost—that is, the regulator treats E as a *fixed cost*. Then, the relative markup condition will appear differently,

$$\frac{(P_1-MC_1)/P_1}{(P_2-(1-a)MC_2)/P_2} = \frac{1/\eta_1}{1/\eta_2}. \qquad (6.10)$$

In other words, the markup over marginal cost for the second product will be exaggerated because the attributable marginal cost is incorrectly reduced. One would generally expect this to result in a relatively lower price for product 2 and a correspondingly higher price for product 1. Sufficient shifting of attributable cost to joint and common cost will yield cross-subsidies' going from product 1 to product 2.

Misallocation of attributable cost to joint and common cost can create cross-subsidies even with traditional fully distributed cost allocation rules. A simple example illustrates this possibility. Suppose that the output levels are measured in terms of some common unit, such as number of pieces of mail. Then the shares of fixed joint and common costs that are allocated to products 1 and 2, respectively, are $Q_1/(Q_1+Q_2)$ and $Q_2/(Q_1+Q_2)$. The rates assigned to the two classes, R_1 and R_2, are then derived in the standard manner:

$$R_1 = [\frac{Q_1}{(Q_1+Q_2)}][F+aC_2(Q_2)]+C_1(Q_1) \qquad (6.11)$$

$$R_2 = [\frac{Q_2}{(Q_1+Q_2)}][F+aC_2(Q_2)]+(1-a)C_2(Q_2). \qquad (6.12)$$

The sum of those two amounts fully recovers the firm's total cost. For the rate structure to be free of cross-subsidies, it must also be the case that revenues do not exceed stand-alone costs, $R_1 \leq F+C_1(Q_1)$ and $R_2 \leq F+C_2(Q_2)$.

Those requirements can easily fail to hold. In particular, product 1 is providing a subsidy if the cost-shifting parameter is sufficiently large,

$$a > \frac{F/Q_1}{C_2(Q_2)/Q_2}.$$

For any cost-shifting parameter a, that cross-subsidy condition is more likely to apply if any of the following conditions exist: (1) the actual joint and common costs F are relatively small; (2) the volume of the protected monopoly product 1 is sufficiently large; or (3) the unit cost of the product with a competitive substitute is sufficiently high.

7

Policy Recommendations

HOW SHALL CONGRESS respond to the Postal Service's call for reduced regulatory controls and greater flexibility to compete with private companies? Our analysis implies that Congress has four alternatives: acquiesce, privatize, commercialize, or strengthen public oversight. Of those four, commercialization is most attractive in terms of being a politically feasible option that would appreciably enhance economic welfare.

ACQUIESCENCE

Our discussion of the Postal Service's privileges, performance, and objectives explains why it is inadvisable on public policy grounds for Congress to acquiesce to the Postal Service's plans to expand its activities in and into competitive markets ably served by private firms. Continued Postal Service expansion threatens not only parcel post and express mail carriers, but also newspapers, commercial mailing services, and local delivery companies. Acquiescence to the Postal Service's call for looser regulatory controls will remove existing safeguards without such counterbalancing constraints as explicit and effective antitrust scrutiny, private ownership, or competition in the delivery of letters.

The express mail market is served by many carriers, including Federal Express, United Parcel Service, Airborne, and Emery/Purolator. Federal Express, with over $8 billion in sales, provides domestic and international services and has the largest fleet of air cargo delivery planes in the world.[1] United Parcel Service, with over $19 billion in sales, provides a full range of ground and air delivery services. In 1994 Airborne Freight earned nearly $2 billion in revenues and Air Express International nearly $1 billion.

The market for parcel delivery is served by numerous companies, including Consolidated Freightways, Inc., DHL Worldwide Express, United Parcel Service, Roadway Services, and Pittston. Consolidated Freightways, with over $4 billion in revenues, operates Con-Way, which offers overnight and second-day delivery. Emery Worldwide is the leading heavy-freight air carrier in the United States, and it is also a Postal Service contractor, because it carries priority mail for the Postal Service.[2] Roadway Services, with over $14 billion in revenues, is the largest provider of less-than-truckload services through its Roadway Express subsidiary.[3] Pittston has revenues exceeding $2.5 billion.

In August 1995—less than three weeks after Alternate Postal Delivery, Inc., filed a registration statement for an initial public offering[4]—the Postal Service announced a test of

---

1. HOOVER'S HANDBOOK OF AMERICAN BUSINESS 1995, at 488-89 (Gary Hoover, Alta Campbell & Patrick J. Spain eds., The Reference Press 1995).
2. *Id.* at 388-89.
3. *Id.* at 922-23.
4. ALTERNATE POSTAL DELIVERY, INC., REGISTRATION STATEMENT FOR INITIAL PUBLIC OFFERING OF 1,000,000 SHARES OF COMMON STOCK (Aug.

a new service of local delivery called "neighborhood mail" in which advertisers could pay for the delivery of commercial circulars to every residence on specific routes.[5] Advertisers would not need to obtain mailing lists, because they could simply target mail delivery routes. Those advertisers would need only to print "postal patron" or "neighbor" on their correspondence. This proposed service is of concern to several types of companies. Newspapers derive a significant share of their revenues from local advertising. The Postal Service's proposed service would likely divert advertising revenues that newspapers receive from local merchants. According to the Postal Service, "neighborhood mail" would target such local establishments as pizza businesses, dry cleaners, florists, and hardware stores.[6] The president of the National Newspaper Association reacted to the "neighborhood mail" proposal by stating that "the Postal Service has lost its way" and "think[s] [that it is] in the advertising business."[7] Moreover, "neighborhood mail" would compete with newspaper carriers that deliver some forms of unaddressed advertising mail, and it would reduce demand for the large mail-advertising industry, which develops and sells mailing lists to advertisers. The affected companies would include Harte-Hanks Communications, Inc., Advo, Inc., Mailmen, Inc., Mid-America Mailers, Inc., and Lee DataMail Services. The proposed service would further affect bulk mailers, such as Harte-Hanks. In response to complaints from private firms, the Postal Service decided to postpone the test of this new service.[8]

2, 1995).

5. Bill McAllister, *Special Delivery for "Junk Mail,"* WASH. POST, Aug. 18, 1995, at A1.

6. Asra Q. Nomani, *Newspapers, Direct-Mail Firms Blast Postal Service's New Plan for Fliers*, WALL ST. J., Aug. 2, 1994, at A2.

7. McAllister, *supra* note 5 (quoting Tonda F. Rush).

8. *Postal Service Delays Test of New Bulk Mail Delivery*, WALL ST. J., Aug. 31, 1995, at A10.

The Postal Service also has considered providing access to the information superhighway. The introduction of such services would bring the Postal Service into competition with Internet access providers and telecommunications companies. The Postal Service is also contemplating entry into electronic mail delivery and certification systems, again to compete with telecommunications providers.[9] In addition, it is contemplating entry into "electronic commerce," thereby competing with banks and other financial institutions, telecommunications firms, and computer software companies.[10]

Consistent with those forays into competitive markets, Postmaster General Runyon takes an expansive view of the Postal Service's potential markets: "[T]here is no longer any question that in messaging, advertising, publications and funds transfer—*all core businesses of ours*—change is occurring."[11] The Postal Service is straying far from its original mission. Its efforts to diversify into markets that are effectively served by broad segments of U.S. industry should raise concern in Congress because such diversification brings the federal government into competition with the private sector in an unprecedented manner. The Postal Service no longer seeks to plug gaps in the provision of public services. Rather, it seeks to divert business from private firms in existing and emerging industries.

The General Accounting Office, the postmaster general, and the Postal Service have recommended that, while retaining its statutory monopoly over letter mail, the Postal Service receive greater latitude to cut prices for those postal services that private firms currently provide on a competitive

---

9. U.S. POSTAL SERV., 1994 ANNUAL REP. 10 (1995); Christy Fisher, *An Interactive Stamp of Approval: Postal Service Bets on New Media to Stave off Electronic Competition*, ADVERTISING AGE, June 20, 1994.

10. U.S. POSTAL SERV., 1994 ANNUAL REP. 10 (1995).

11. Address by Postmaster General Marvin Runyon to the National Press Club, Washington, D.C., July 8, 1993 (emphasis added).

basis. Rather than subject this government-owned enterprise to the rigors of competition over all classes of mail, the GAO, the postmaster general, and the Postal Service would, if their recommendations were followed, increase both the incentive and the opportunity for the Postal Service to engage in anticompetitive cross-subsidization of its provision of competitive services.

As our analysis in chapter 6 demonstrated, the Postal Service would accomplish that result in two steps. First, it would continue to distort and misallocate the attributable costs of providing competitive service by characterizing those costs instead as institutional costs that should be spread across all classes of mail according to Ramsey pricing principles. Second, the Postal Service would distort the inverse elasticity rule, which follows from Ramsey pricing analysis, and would overstate the proportions of the institutional costs of the Postal Service that should be allocated to first class mail. That overallocation of institutional costs to first class mail occurs and would continue to occur because the price elasticity of demand that the Postal Service estimates for first class mail fails to control for the fact that a statutory barrier to entry artificially prevents competitive firms from entering the delivery of letter mail under any circumstances, even when the Postal Service sets a price for that service far in excess of marginal cost. The Postal Service's inference of price inelastic demand for first class mail is the direct consequence of the monopoly this public enterprise enjoys.

For those reasons, we conclude that on grounds of economic welfare the least defensible choice that Congress could make concerning the Postal Service would be to acquiesce to its proclivity for mission creep and empire building.

Privatization

Privatization is the opposite pole on the spectrum of choices facing Congress. If Congress privatized the Postal Service and repealed the Private Express Statutes, the problems of anticompetitive cross-subsidization would eventually disappear. The Postal Service's reservoir of monopoly rents earned from letter mail would dry up and would thus deny the firm the ability to cross-subsidize competitive services. Privatization would force the Postal Service to maximize profits rather than employment or some other objective, and competition would force this multiproduct firm to adopt subsidy-free prices for its various services.[12]

If privatization is so beneficial, why did Congress not choose that option years ago? The answer concerns politics more than economics. Some influential constituencies no doubt believe that a privatized Postal Service would reduce their economic welfare. Those groups presumably include mailers who believe that they currently receive services at prices less than what private firms would have to charge; mail customers in high-cost areas, who fear that their quality of service would deteriorate under private provision of mail delivery; and several hundred thousand postal workers, who fear lower wages and layoffs following privatization. It does not advance the cause of postal reform to advocate privatization of the Postal Service, in lieu of other measures, if the political economy of the situation is such that Congress has calculated that it cannot afford to take so revolutionary a step.

COMMERCIALIZATION

A public enterprise can be commercialized even if it is never privatized. The legal and economic analysis in our preceding chapters suggests that a plan for the commercialization of the Postal Service should include three main elements: removal of

---

12. For a thoughtful discussion of the practical business steps that would be required to privatize the Postal Service, see Bert Ely, *Privatizing the Postal Service: Why Do It; How to Do It*, in FREE THE MAIL: ENDING THE POSTAL MONOPOLY 117 (Peter Ferrara ed., Cato Institute 1990).

statutory entry barriers and other privileges, relief from incumbent burdens, and explicit antitrust oversight. In addition, Congress could profit from studying the efforts of other countries to commercialize their public enterprises.

Repeal the Private Express Statutes and Other Statutory Privileges

Congress should repeal the Private Express Statutes. The general rule in the American economy is that attempted monopolization is a crime, but when it comes to delivering letters it is attempted competition that is the crime. If the Postal Service wishes to compete on the merits with private firms, it should not be allowed to do so behind the protection of a statutory monopoly.

Congress should also repeal the statute that creates the Postal Service's monopoly over access to the customer's mailbox. The repeal of legal restrictions on access to mailboxes by competitors of the Postal Service would properly treat the customer's mailbox as the private property that it is. The deregulation of mailbox access would increase competition across various existing and future classes of mail by lowering costs for competitors of the Postal Service and lowering the consumer's cost of switching from the Postal Service to a private express firm. Open access to the customer's mailbox would permit the development of innovative features, as has occurred with the deregulation of customer premises equipment in telecommunications. Eliminating that small but widespread entry barrier would facilitate competitive services and increase customer convenience.

More generally, Congress should specify by statute that, for as long as the Postal Service remains publicly owned, it shall be subject to all laws generally applicable to private firms and shall have no special privileges or immunities arising from its public ownership. The Postal Service should be subject to all of the antitrust, employment, environmental, securities, tax, and other laws with which any private company must comply. The Postal Service should not be allowed to borrow from the Treasury, nor should its debt be backed by the full faith and credit of the U.S. government.

Relieve the Postal Service of Its Universal Service Obligation and Other Incumbent Burdens

If the Postal Service is to be stripped of its unique statutory privileges as a condition of being allowed to compete freely against private firms, it should also be relieved of its unique statutory obligations. The most conspicuous of those obligations is the universal provision of mail delivery at a uniform price. There are other incumbent burdens, such as law enforcement responsibilities relating to mail fraud, which we have not examined in this book but which should be transferred to other parts of the federal government.

There is a powerful efficiency-based argument for removing the incumbent burdens of the Postal Service, an argument distinct from concerns about symmetry or fairness. As a matter of political economy, it would be easier to repeal the Private Express Statutes and to remove the other barriers to competition in postal services if Congress were simultaneously to remove the putative justification for those special privileges. Because universal service is the most prominent of the Postal Service's incumbent burdens, it is also the Postal Service's last line of defense of the Private Express Statutes.

From the perspective of maximizing consumer welfare, of course, it would be regrettable if the commitment to providing mail service to rural and other high-cost segments of the population were to have the effect of denying *all* segments of the population the substantial benefits that would flow from having multiple providers of letter mail service rather than only one provider. There is also a jurisprudential argument against funding universal service or other incumbent burdens through the creation of artificial monopolies. The cross-subsidies in postal rates are an implicit regime of taxes and appropriations. Taxing and spending is properly the role of Congress under Article I of the Constitution.[13] Congress should not delegate those decisions to the Postal Rate Commission and the Postal Service—neither of which has any direct political accountability to the electorate. The magnitude of the subsidy to rural recipients of mail should be apparent from an explicit line item in the budget; it should not be an amount that can be inferred only by undertaking extensive economic analysis of the cross-subsidies effected by the monopoly over letter mail.

Despite the repeated efforts of scholars to convey those messages in a variety of regulated industries, including postal delivery, rate structures containing cross-subsidies have endured in such industries. If one hopes to influence public policy in the real world, it is therefore necessary to take account of how actual political constituencies and institutions may prevent the achievement of reforms that would increase economic welfare. By enacting legislation to fund universal postal service in a way that does not depend on the artificial creation of a monopoly, Congress would deny opponents of postal commercialization their most politically effective argument for not repealing the Private Express Statutes and the Postal Service's other special privileges.

There are at least two general means by which Congress could decouple universal service from the Private Express Statutes. First, Congress could send postal subsidies directly to consumers in rural areas. Those subsidies could even be means-tested, if one's low income were considered to be more important than one's rural address. Those customers would then be billed directly by the carrier of last resort for the high cost of what might be called "terminating access," to

---

13. U.S. CONST. art. I, § 8, cl. 1, § 9, cl. 7.

borrow a telecommunications concept. The lower basic stamp price that would result would not include the surcharge for delivery to costly, remote areas. A second means would be for the government to solicit bids from private firms to deliver mail to remote areas for a specified contract term. The winning bid would be that which proposed to provide service at the lowest subsidy from the government. If Congress were to adopt either approach, it could end the false rhetoric that American consumers must tolerate a monopoly to have universal service.

Subject the Postal Service to Explicit Antitrust Oversight

The Postal Service's history of suppressing competition in letter mail, and its use in 1993 and 1994 of its search and seizure powers to dissuade large business customers from using Federal Express for mail that the Postal Service did not regard as "extremely urgent," suggest that competition would not come naturally to this public enterprise. In its current form, however, the Postal Rate Commission is not up to the task of regulating the Postal Service in a manner that would protect its efficient private competitors. It is a recognized danger that an industry-specific regulator will become captured by the companies it regulates.[14] The Postal Rate Commission faces this risk with three additional handicaps. First, it is not merely an industry-specific regulator, but a firm-specific one. Even in the days of the Bell System, the Federal Communications Commission's agenda was not dictated by AT&T alone. Second, the Postal Service in effect has by statute the right to disregard the Postal Rate Commission's decisions. Third, the Postal Rate Commission is fundamentally

---

14. George J. Stigler, *The Theory of Economic Regulation*, 2 BELL J. ECON. & MGMT. SCI. 137 (1971).

a ratemaking body expert in issues of revenue adequacy and fairness across classes of customers, not an antitrust enforcer expert in measuring competition and assessing the effect of strategic behavior on consumer welfare.

Congress should therefore explicitly subject the Postal Service to the antitrust laws and to the competitive oversight of the Antitrust Division of the Department of Justice and the Federal Trade Commission. Those agencies have expertise in competitive analysis. Furthermore, they have independence because they enforce statutes that apply to all industries. Finally, the Antitrust Division in particular has special experience in dealing with antitrust problems concerning regulated network industries bearing some similarity to the postal industry, such as telecommunications.

Learn from Commercialization in Other Countries

Relative to other Western democracies, the United States historically has had relatively few publicly owned business enterprises. Consequently, the United States is relatively inexperienced in "denationalizing" such public enterprises. Other nations may therefore provide Congress with useful lessons for the commercialization of the Postal Service.

For example, Congress might examine Telstra Corporation Limited, a telecommunications company with annual revenues exceeding $13 billion (Australian).[15] The Australian government owns Telstra and is represented on its board of directors by the minister for communications and the arts.[16] Despite Telstra's public ownership, the company faces not only competition, but also the ordinary legal obligations of any private corporation, including taxation, financial disclo-

---

15. TELSTRA CORP. LTD., 1994 ANNUAL REP. at inner cover (1994).
16. *Id.*

sure, and conformity with antitrust statutes. Telstra paid over $800 million (Australian) in taxes in fiscal year 1994.[17] It also paid the Australian government a dividend of $738 million (Australian).[18] Telstra's annual report for 1994 contains thirty-four pages of detailed financial statements and notes,[19] compared with twenty-one pages in the Postal Service's 1994 annual report and eleven pages in its 1994 "comprehensive" statement on operations.[20] Under the current wireline duopoly in Australia, Telstra faces competition from Optus Communications Limited, which is 49 percent owned by two large foreign telecommunications firms, BellSouth Corporation and Cable & Wireless plc.[21] Telstra is subject to antitrust laws and specific competition legislation concerning telecommunications.[22] Indeed, in March 1993, Optus sued Telstra on the grounds that its pricing and product bundling of long-distance services for large customers were anticompetitive.[23]

Telstra is not an isolated example of a commercialized public enterprise. The largest telephone company in the world, Nippon Telegraph and Telephone, though still substantially owned by the Japanese government, pays taxes and dividends and is subject to the Telecommunications Business Law, which requires that the Japanese telecommunications

---

17. *Id.* at 39.
18. *Id.* at 5.
19. *Id.* at 30–63.
20. U.S. POSTAL SERV., 1994 ANNUAL REP. 17–37 (1995); U.S. POSTAL SERVICE, COMPREHENSIVE STATEMENT ON POSTAL OPERATIONS, FY 1994, at 37–47 (1995) [hereinafter 1994 COMPREHENSIVE STATEMENT].
21. BELLSOUTH CORP., 1994 SEC FORM 10-K, at 11 (1995); CABLE & WIRELESS PLC, 1994 SEC FORM 20-F, at 38 (1994). Australian law provides that the current duopoly will be opened to full competition in 1997. MINISTRY FOR COMMUNICATIONS AND THE ARTS, BEYOND THE DUOPOLY: AUSTRALIAN TELECOMMUNICATIONS POLICY AND REGULATION (1994).
22. *Id.* at 33.
23. TELSTRA CORP. LTD., 1994 ANNUAL REP. 51 (1994).

services industry be open to competition.[24] Prominent examples such as Telstra and NTT raise the embarrassing question of why Congress has never subjected the publicly owned Postal Service to all of the same laws that its private competitors must obey. At the same time, these large foreign companies are evidence that, even in countries far more accustomed than the United States to direct government participation in the production of goods and services, commercialization is a feasible political strategy, either as an end in itself or as an intermediate step toward eventual privatization.

STRICTER PUBLIC OVERSIGHT

If commercialization of the Postal Service is not politically feasible along the lines that we have just described, then Congress must select the remaining option of substantially increasing public oversight of the Postal Service. That option contains four necessary elements. One is to enlarge the powers of the Postal Rate Commission and make it truly an independent body. The second is to disabuse the Postal Service of any notion that its mission is to earn "profit" for the federal government. The third is strictly to limit the lines of business in which the Postal Service may operate. The fourth is to subject the Postal Service to explicit antitrust oversight to ensure that it does not abuse its continuing privileges under the Private Express Statutes and other laws.

Strengthen the Postal Rate Commission

If the Private Express Statutes remain and the Postal Service retains its other statutory privileges as a public enterprise, then the Congress must give the Postal Rate Commission the

---

24. NIPPON TELEGRAPH & TELEPHONE CORP. (NIPPON DENSHIN DENWA KABUSHIKI KAISHA), 1994 SEC FORM 20-F/A, at 2–3, F-20 (1994).

same powers and credibility that agencies such as the Federal Communications Commission and the Federal Energy Regulatory Commission have with respect to the private firms that they regulate. At a minimum, such legislation would have to eliminate the Postal Service's ability to overrule the rate recommendations of the Postal Rate Commission. In addition, the Postal Rate Commission would need to have the authority to impose its own accounting standards on the Postal Service, to require the Postal Service's routine reporting of reliable cost data, and to order whatever structural relief (such as divestiture of operating units, separate subsidiaries, accounting separations, and so forth) it deemed necessary to regulate the Postal Service in a manner that advanced the purposes of public provision of postal services.

Clarify That It Is Not the Postal Service's Mission to Be a "Profit Center" for the Federal Government

If the Postal Service is not commercialized, Congress should reject the Postmaster General's call to make the Postal Service a "profit center" for the federal government. Even taken at face value, that proposed mission is especially questionable in light of the many reasons that exist to conclude that the Postal Service currently does not act as a profit maximizer.

The economic justification for public enterprise is either that there is a natural monopoly or that there is an externality. Neither is present in the case of postal services, or at least present in sufficient magnitude to necessitate public ownership as the form of government intervention. Economic theory does not justify public enterprise on the ground that the government can make a profit competing against private firms. The government's source of funds is better confined to its taxation of the private economic activity of firms and households.

Remove the Postal Service from Markets That Are Demonstrably Competitive

In any market where private firms already provide adequate mail services, there is no need for the Postal Service. Congress should remove the Postal Service by statute from any such market, or delegate such removal power to the Postal Rate Commission, for no market failure is present that could justify government intervention, let alone intervention in the extreme form of a publicly owned enterprise. The antitrust laws are sufficient to ensure that postal markets that are demonstrably competitive today will not be monopolized or cartelized by private firms when the Postal Service exits the field.

Moreover, the process of removing the Postal Service from competitive markets would help to establish one or more additional private competitors. For example, the assets that the Postal Service uses to provide overnight mail service in competition with Federal Express, United Parcel Service, and other private firms obviously would not evaporate if Congress were to remove the Postal Service from that market. The Postal Service has twenty-nine aircraft and a hub in Indianapolis that it uses to deliver express mail.[25] Before resorting to piecemeal liquidation of those aircraft and hub assets, the government surely would explore with its investment banker the possibility of selling express mail intact as a viable product line. Potential buyers would include the smaller package and freight companies and the airlines. If no buyer could be found for express mail as a going concern, that fact would powerfully imply that the Postal Service wastes resources when it provides overnight mail service.

---

25. 1994 COMPREHENSIVE STATEMENT, *supra* note 20, at 13.

Explicitly Subject Abuses of the Private Express Statutes to the Antitrust Laws

Even if Congress declined to repeal the Private Express Statutes, there would still be a role for review of the Postal Service by the Antitrust Division or the Federal Trade Commission. Such review would determine whether the Postal Service was using its lawful monopoly over letter mail to reduce competition in markets for other services. In principle, this role for the antitrust agencies would resemble the Antitrust Division's frequent examination under the Modification of Final Judgment of whether a particular regional Bell operating company (upon which state law may continue to confer a statutory monopoly over local exchange service) is using that lawful monopoly to reduce competition in a different product market, such as long-distance service, that the regional Bell operating company seeks to enter or in which it already operates. This form of antitrust oversight would be the natural complement to an order by the Postal Rate Commission removing the Postal Service from demonstrably competitive markets.

CONCLUSION

The path to more competitive and innovative mail service in the United States is not to facilitate predatory cross-subsidization by a government-owned monopolist. In other words, the proper policy is not one of congressional acquiescence to the unconstrained diversification and corporate aggrandizement of the Postal Service.

Rather, the policy most conducive to greater economic welfare is one of commercialization of the Postal Service. Such a reform package would repeal the Private Express Statutes and other statutory privileges enjoyed by the Postal Service, explicitly subject the Postal Service to the antitrust laws and all other laws of general applicability to private businesses, and relieve the Postal Service of its incumbent burdens, including the duty to deliver at a uniform national rate to high-cost areas. The Postal Rate Commission would oversee the transition to competition and then cease to exist. This set of reforms might eventually lead to the privatization of the Postal Service, though it need not. Indeed, privatization would be unconscionable on economic grounds if it failed to provide for repeal of the Private Express Statutes.

If, on the other hand, Congress declines to commercialize the Postal Service, its remaining option will be considerably more invasive. The Postal Service's continued enjoyment of statutory privileges will necessitate much greater oversight of the Postal Service by the Postal Rate Commission, the Postal Service's divestiture of operations in demonstrably competitive lines of business, and close antitrust oversight to ensure that the Postal Service does not abuse its lawful monopoly over letter mail.

The least acceptable course of action is for Congress to continue to do nothing in the face of the Postal Service's expanding empire. The postmaster general's observation that the Postal Service could become a profit center for the federal government is an admission that it is time for Congress to protect competition from the postal monopoly.

References

Adie, Douglas K., "How Have the Postal Workers Fared Since the 1970 Act?," in *Perspectives on Postal Service Issues* 74 (Roger Sherman ed., AEI Press 1980).

Airborne Freight, 1994 *SEC Form 10-K* (1995).

Alberta, Paul M., "Probers Find Mail Stashed in Trailers," *DM News*, July 25, 1994, at 3.

Alternate Postal Delivery, Inc., *Registration Statement for Initial Public Offering of 1,000,000 Shares of Common Stock* (Aug. 2, 1995).

American Freightways, 1994 *SEC Form 10-K* (1995).

Baumol, William J., *Superfairness: Applications and Theory* (MIT Press 1986).

Baumol, William J., "Ramsey Pricing," in 4 *The New Palgrave: A Dictionary of Economics* 49 (John Eatwell, Murray Milgate & Peter Newman eds., MacMillan Press Limited 1987).

Baumol, William J., and David F. Bradford, "Optimal Departures from Marginal Cost Pricing," 60 *American Economic Review* 265 (1970).

Baumol, William J., and J. Gregory Sidak, "Stranded Costs," 18 *Harvard Journal of Law and Public Policy* 835 (1995).

Baumol, William J., and J. Gregory Sidak, *Toward Competition in Local Telephony* (MIT Press and AEI Press 1994).

Baumol, William J., and J. Gregory Sidak, *Transmission Pricing and Stranded Costs in the Electric Power Industry* (AEI Press 1995).

Baumol, William J., and Robert D. Willig, "Fixed Cost, Sunk Cost, Entry Barriers and Sustainability of Monopoly," 95 *Quarterly Journal of Economics* 405 (1981).

Baumol, William J., John C. Panzar, and Robert D. Willig, *Contestable Markets and the Theory of Industry Structure* (Harcourt Brace Jovanovich 1982; rev. ed. 1988).

BellSouth Corp., 1994 *SEC Form 10-K* (1995).

Berg, Sanford V., and John Tschirhart, *Natural Monopoly Regulation: Principles and Practice* (Cambridge University Press 1988).

BeVier, Lillian R., "Rehabilitating the Public Forum Doctrine: In Defense of Categories," 1994 *Supreme Court Review* 79.

Bowles, Scott, and Toni Locy, "Discovered Mail May Be Delayed or Not Delivered," *Washington Post,* Oct. 20, 1994, at C3.

Braeutigam, Ronald R., and John C. Panzar, "Diversification Incentives Under 'Price-Based' and 'Cost-Based' Regulation," 20 *RAND Journal of Economics* 373 (1989).

Braeutigam, Ronald R., and John C. Panzar, "Effects of the Change from Rate-of-Return to Price-Cap Regulation," 83 *American Economic Review Papers and Proceedings* 191 (1993).

"Bush Reportedly Threatens Postal Board over Rate Rise," *New York Times*, Jan. 5, 1993, at A11.

"Bush Temporarily Prevented from Dismissing Postmaster," *New York Times*, Jan. 8, 1993, at A13.

Cable & Wireless plc, 1994 *SEC Form 20-F* (1994).

Carlton, Dennis W., and Jeffrey M. Perloff, *Modern Industrial Organization* (Harper Collins 2d ed. 1994).

Castaneda, Ruben, and Linda Wheeler, "Dead, Ailing Animals Found in D.C. Postal Worker's Home: Allegedly Stolen Mail Also in NW Apartment," *Washington Post,* Oct. 19, 1994, at B1.

Chandler, Alfred D., *Scale and Scope: The Dynamics of Industrial Capitalism* (Harvard University Press 1990).

Chronis, Peter G., "Crucial Postal Machinery Cited by OSHA for Injuries," *Denver Post*, May 20, 1995, at B3.

Coase, Ronald H., "Rowland Hill and the Penny Post," 6 *Economica* 423 (n.s. 1939).

Coase, Ronald H., "The Postal Monopoly in Great Britain: An Historical Survey," in *Economic Essays in Commemoration of the Dundee School of Economics 1931-1955* (J.K. Eastham ed. 1955).

Coase, Ronald H., "The British Post Office and the Messenger Companies," 4 *Journal of Law and Economics* 12 (1961).

Consolidated Freightways, Inc., 1994 *SEC Form 10-K* (1995).

Corporate Profile for DHL Express, Business Wire, Inc. (Sept. 9, 1994).

Costich, Rand, and Gail Willette, "Regulation of Unregulated Firms: The Postal Service and UPS," in *Commercialization of Postal and Delivery Services: National and International Perspectives* 237 (Michael A. Crew and Paul R. Kleindorfer eds., Kluwer Academic Publishers 1994).

"Court Blocks Dismissal of Postal Governors," *New York Times*, Jan. 17, 1993, at I22.

Crandall, Robert W., *After the Breakup: Telecommunications in a More Competitive Era* (Brookings Institution 1991).

Crew, Michael A., and Paul R. Kleindorfer, *The Economics of Postal Service* (Kluwer Academic Publishers 1992).

Crew, Michael A., and Paul R. Kleindorfer, "Pricing, Entry, Service Quality, and Innovation under a Commercialized Postal Service," in *Governing the Postal Service* 150 (J. Gregory Sidak ed., AEI Press 1994).

Cullinan, Gerald, *The Post Office Department* (Frederick A. Praeger 1968).

Davis, O. A., and A. B. Whinston, "Welfare Economics and the Theory of Second Best," 32 *Review of Economic Studies* 1 (1965).

Devins, Neal, "Tempest in an Envelope: Reflections on the Bush White House's Failed Takeover of the U.S. Postal Service," 41 *UCLA Law Review* 1035 (1994).

Ely, Bert, "Privatizing the Postal Service: Why Do It; How to Do It," in *Free the Mail: Ending the Postal Monopoly* (Peter Ferrara ed., Cato Institute 1990).

Federal Express Corp., 1994 *SEC Form 10-K* (1994).

Feldstein, Martin S., "Distributional Equity and the Optimal Structure of Public Prices," 62 *American Economic Review* 32 (1972).

Feldstein, Martin S., "Equity and Efficiency in Public Sector Pricing: The Optimal Two-Part Tariff," 86 *Quarterly Journal of Economics* 175 (1972).

"Firemen Find Sacks of Mail," *New York Times*, May 10, 1994, at 12.

Fisher, Christy, "An Interactive Stamp of Approval: Postal Service Bets on New Media to Stave off Electronic Competition," *Advertising Age*, June 20, 1994.

"The *Fortune* 500 Largest U.S. Companies," *Fortune*, May 15, 1995, at 165.

Franzen, Jonathan, "Lost in the Mail," *The New Yorker*, Oct. 24, 1994, at 62.

Fuller, Wayne E., *The American Mail: Enlarger of the Common Life* (University of Chicago Press 1972).

Fuss, Melvyn A., "Cost Allocation: How Can the Costs of Postal Services Be Determined?," in *Perspectives on Postal Service Issues* 30 (Roger Sherman ed., AEI Press 1980).

Geddes, R. Richard, "Agency Costs and Governance in the United States Postal Service," in *Governing the Postal Service* 114 (J. Gregory Sidak ed., AEI Press 1994).

General Accounting Office, *Postal Service: Automation Is Taking Longer and Producing Less Than Expected* (1995).

General Accounting Office, *U.S. Postal Pricing: Pricing Postal Services in a Competitive Environment* (1992).

Governing the Postal Service (J. Gregory Sidak ed., AEI Press 1994).

Greyhound Lines, Inc., 1994 *SEC Form 10-K* (1995).

Haldi, John, *Postal Monopoly: An Assessment of the Private Express Statutes* (AEI Press 1974).

Hall, George R., "Regulatory Systems for Postal Rates," in *Regulation and the Nature of Postal and Delivery Services* 221 (Michael A. Crew and Paul R. Kleindorfer eds., Kluwer Academic Publishers 1993).

Hansmann, Henry B., "The Postal Service as a Public Enterprise: Commentary," in *Governing the Postal Service* 39 (J. Gregory Sidak ed., AEI Press 1994).

"Hearings Before the Subcommittee on the Postal Service of the House Committee on Government Reform and Oversight," 104th Congress, 1st Session (June 14, 1995).

Hiltzik, Michael A., "Postal Agency Faces Fight with High-Tech Rivals," *Los Angeles Times*, Dec. 16, 1994, at A1.

Hoover's Handbook of American Business 1995 (Gary Hoover, Alta Campbell, and Patrick J. Spain eds., The Reference Press 1995).

Houston, Paul, and Robert Shogan, "Washington Insight," *Los Angeles Times*, Apr. 4, 1994, at A5.

Hyman, Leonard S., *America's Electric Utilities: Past, Present and Future* (Public Utilities Reports, Inc. 5th ed. 1994).

Institute for Public Administration, *The Ratemaking Process for the United States Postal Service* (report to the Board of Governors of the U.S. Postal Service, Oct. 1991).

Jensen, Michael C., "Agency Costs of Free Cash Flow, Corporate Finance, and Takeovers," 76 *American Economic Review Papers and Proceedings* 323 (1986).

Kahn, Alfred E., *The Economics of Regulation* (MIT Press rev. ed. 1988).

Karpoff, Jonathan M., and John R. Lott, Jr., "The Reputational Penalty Firms Bear from Committing Criminal Fraud," 36 *Journal of Law and Economics* 757 (1993).

Kellogg, Michael K., John Thorne, and Peter W. Huber, *Federal Telecommunications Law* (Little, Brown & Co. 1992).

Klein, Benjamin, and Keith B. Leffler, "The Role of Market Forces in Assuring Contractual Performance," 89 *Journal of Political Economy* 615 (1981).

Landes, William E., and Richard A. Posner, "Market Power in Antitrust Cases," 94 *Harvard Law Review* 937 (1981).

Lerner, Abba P., "On Optimal Taxes with an Untaxable Sector," 60 *American Economic Review* 284 (1970).

"Letters Outside of the Mails Carried by Railroad Companies—Statutory Construction," 21 *Opinions of the Attorney General* 394 (1886).

Lewis, Tracy R., and David E. M. Sappington, "Regulatory Options and Price Cap Regulation," 20 *RAND Journal of Economics* 405 (1989).

McAllister, Bill, "Millions of Letters Undelivered; Local Facilities Held Unprocessed Mail," *Washington Post*, July 20, 1994, at A1.

McAllister, Bill, "Must It Get There Overnight?" *Washington Post*, Jan. 12, 1994, at A17.

McAllister, Bill, "Post Office Acts to End Backlog; Overtime Is Ordered for Area Mail Clerks Today and Sunday," *Washington Post*, July 23, 1994, at A1.

McAllister, Bill, "Postal Service Drops Promise on 2-Day Mail; Runyon Also Orders Halt to Raiding of Businesses," *Washington Post*, Mar. 25, 1994, at A21.

McAllister, Bill, "Special Delivery for 'Junk Mail'," *Washington Post*, Aug. 18, 1995, at A1.

MacAvoy, Paul W., *Industry Regulation and the Performance of the American Economy* (W.W. Norton & Co. 1992).

MacAvoy, Paul W., and George S. McIsaac, "The Current File on the Case for Privatization of the Federal Government Enterprises," 4 *Hume Papers on Public Policy* (forthcoming 1995).

MacAvoy, Paul W., Daniel F. Spulber, and Bruce E. Stangle, "Is Competitive Entry Free?: Bypass and Partial Deregulation in Natural Gas Markets," 6 *Yale Journal on Regulation* 209 (1989).

Mail Boxes Etc., 1994 *SEC Form 10-K* (1994).

Makovic, Eugene, "Time for Postal Competition," *St. Louis Post-Dispatch*, July 21, 1994, at 7B.

Maloney, Michael T., and Mark L. Mitchell, "Crisis in the Cockpit? The Role of Market Forces in Promoting Air Travel Safety," 32 *Journal of Law and Economics* 329 (1989).

Mayton, William Ty, "The Mission and Methods of the Postal Service," in *Governing the Postal Service* 60 (J. Gregory Sidak ed., AEI Press 1994).

Milgrom, Paul, and John Roberts, *Economics, Organization and Management* (Prentice Hall 1992).

Mill, John Stuart, *Principles of Political Economy* (John W. Parker 1848).

Miller, Bill, "Post Offices Playing Catch-up; Workers on Overtime to Speed up Delivery," *Washington Post*, July 24, 1994, at B1.

Ministry for Communications and the Arts, *Beyond the Duopoly: Australian Telecommunications Policy and Regulation* (1994).

Mitchell, Bridger M., and Ingo Vogelsang, *Telecommunications Pricing: Theory and Practice* (Cambridge University Press 1991).

"More Undelivered Mail Found in Chicago," *New York Times*, Apr. 16, 1994, at 6.

Nippon Telegraph & Telephone Corp. (Nippon Denshin Denwa Kabushiki Kaisha), 1994 *SEC Form 20-F/A* (1994).

Nomani, Asra Q., "Newspapers, Direct-Mail Firms Blast Postal Service's New Plan for Fliers," *Wall Street Journal*, Aug. 21, 1995, at A2.

Oster, Sharon M., "The Failure of Postal Reform," 4 *Hume Papers on Public Policy* (forthcoming 1995).

Oster, Sharon M., "The Postal Service as a Public Enterprise," in *Governing the Postal Service* 31 (J. Gregory Sidak ed., AEI Press 1994).

Owen, Bruce M., and Robert D. Willig, "Economics and Postal Pricing," in *The Future of the Postal Service* 227 (Joel L. Fleishman ed., Aspen Institute and Praeger Publishers 1983).

Panzar, John C., "Competition, Efficiency, and the Vertical Structure of Postal Services," in *Regulation and the Nature of Postal Delivery Services* 91 (Michael A. Crew and Paul R. Kleindorfer eds., Kluwer Academic Publishers 1992).

Panzar, John C., "The Economics of Mail Delivery," in *Governing the Postal Service* 1 (J. Gregory Sidak ed., AEI Press 1994).

Panzar, John C., "Is Postal Service a Natural Monopoly?," in *Competition and Innovation in Postal Services* 219 (Michael A. Crew and Paul R. Kleindorfer eds., Kluwer Academic Publishers 1991).

Panzar, John C., and Robert D. Willig, "Economies of Scale in Multi-Output Production," 91 *Quarterly Journal of Economics* 481 (1977).

Perloff, Jeffrey M., and Michael L. Wachter, "A Comparative Analysis of Wage Premiums and Industrial Relations in the British Post Office and the United States Postal Service," in *Competition and Innovation in Postal Services* 115 (Michael A. Crew and Paul R. Kleindorfer eds., Kluwer Academic Publishers 1991).

Phelps, Edith M., "Parcels Post," in *Debaters' Handbook Series* 1 (H. W. Wilson Co. 1913).

"Post Office Sending Agencies a Message," *Chicago Tribune*, Jan. 16, 1994, at 10.

"Postal Service Delays Test of New Bulk Mail Delivery," *Wall Street Journal*, Aug. 31, 1995, at A10.

Priest, George L., "The History of the Postal Monopoly in the United States," 18 *Journal of Law and Economics* 33 (1975).

Priest, George L., "Socialism, Eastern Europe, and the Question of the Postal Monopoly," in *Governing the Postal Service* 46 (J. Gregory Sidak ed., AEI Press 1994).

"Private Couriers and Postal Service Slug It Out," *New York Times*, Feb. 14, 1994, at D1.

Ramsey, Frank P., "A Contribution to the Theory of Taxation," 37 *Economic Journal* 47 (1927).

Roadway Services, Inc., 1994 *SEC Form 10-K* (1995).

Rogerson, Cathy M., and William M. Takis, "Economies of Scale and Scope and Competition in Postal Services, in *Regulation and the Nature of Postal Delivery Services* 109 (Michael A. Crew and Paul R. Kleindorfer eds., Kluwer Academic Publishers 1992).

Runyon, Marvin, Address to the National Postal Forum, Nashville, Tennessee (May 8, 1995).

Runyon, Marvin, Address to the National Press Club, Washington, D.C. (Jan. 31, 1995).

Scott, Frank A., Jr., "The Pricing Policy of the Postal Service: Economics Misapplied," 4 *Journal of Policy Analysis and Management* 251 (1985).

Scott, Frank A., Jr., "Assessing USA Postal Ratemaking: An Application of Ramsey Prices," 34 *Journal of Industrial Economics* 279 (1986).

Sherman, Roger, *The Regulation of Monopoly* (Cambridge University Press 1989).

Sherman, Roger, and Anthony George, "Second-Best Pricing for the U.S. Postal Service," 45 *Southern Economic Journal* 685 (1979).

Sidak, J. Gregory, "The Economics of Mail Delivery: Commentary," in *Governing the Postal Service* 14 (J. Gregory Sidak ed., AEI Press 1994).

Sidak, J. Gregory, "Telecommunications in Jericho," 81 *California Law Review* 1209 (1993).

Smith, Kerri S., "Post Office Ordered to Start Injury-Prevention Plan," *Rocky Mountain News*, Aug. 3, 1994, at 48A.

Spence, A. Michael, "Regulating the Structural Environment of the Postal Service," in *The Future of the Postal Service* 197 (Joel L. Fleishman ed., Aspen Institute and Praeger Publishers 1983).

Spulber, Daniel F., "Economic Analysis and Management Strategy: A Survey Continued," 3 *Journal of Economics and Management Strategy* 355 (1994).

Spulber, Daniel F., *Regulation and Markets* (MIT Press 1989).

Stigler, George J., "The Division of Labor Is Limited by the Extent of the Market," 59 *Journal of Political Economy* 185 (1951), *reprinted in* George J. Stigler, *The Organization of Industry* (Richard D. Irwin, Inc. 1968).

Stigler, George J., *The Organization of Industry* (Richard D. Irwin, Inc. 1968).

Stigler, George J., "The Theory of Economic Regulation," 2 *Bell Journal of Economics and Management Science* 137 (1971).

Stiglitz, Joseph E., Marius Schwartz, and Eric D. Wolff, *Towards Competition in International Satellite Services: Rethinking the Role of INTELSAT* (Council of Economic Advisers draft, June 1995).

Telstra Corp. Ltd., 1994 *Annual Report* (1994).

Tierney, John T., *The U.S. Postal Service: Status andProspects of a Public Enterprise* (Auburn House 1988).

Time Warner Inc., 1994 *SEC Form 10-K* (1995).

Tirole, Jean, *The Theory of Industrial Organization* (MIT Press 1988).

Train, Kenneth E., *Optimal Regulation: The Economic Theory of Natural Monopoly* (MIT Press 1991).

Tye, William B., "The Postal Service: Economics Made Simplistic," 3 *Journal of Policy Analysis and Management* 62 (1983).

Tye, William B., "The Pricing Policy of the Postal Service: Policymaking Misunderstood," 4 *Journal of Policy Analysis and Management* 256 (1985).

U.S. Department of Justice, *Changing the Private Express Laws: Competitive Alternatives and the U.S. Postal Service* (1977).

U.S. Postal Service, *Annual Report* (various issues).

U.S. Postal Service, *Comprehensive Statement on Postal Operations, FY 1994* (1994).

U.S. Postal Service, *History of the United States Postal Service, 1775–1993* (1993).

U.S. Postal Service, "Summary Description of USPS Development of Costs by Segments and Components," in *Calculating Postal Product Costs* (Dec. 1994).

Vickers, John, and George Yarrow, *Privatization: An Economic Analysis* (MIT Press 1988).

Waverman, Leonard, "Pricing Principles: How Should Postal Rates Be Set?," in *Perspectives on Postal Service Issues* 7 (Roger Sherman ed., AEI Press 1980).

Wheeler, Linda, "New Homes Found for Animals in D.C. Postal Worker's Menagerie," *Washington Post*, Dec. 5, 1994, at D5.

Williamson, Oliver E., *The Economic Institutions of Capitalism* (Free Press 1985).

Case and Regulatory Proceeding Index

Action of the Governors Under 39 U.S.C., Section 3625, and Supporting Record in the Matter of Postal Rate and Fee Increases, Initial Decision, Dkt. No. R74-1 (Postal Rate Commission 1974), 117n

Air Courier Conf. of Am. v. American Postal Workers Union, 498 U.S. 517 (1991), 15-16, 15n, 16n, 17

Associated Third Class Mail Users v. United States Postal Serv., 600 F.2d 824 (D.C. Cir.), cert. denied, 444 U.S. 837 (1979), 12n, 19, 19n

Associated Third Class Mail Users v. United States Postal Serv., 440 F. Supp. 1211 (D.D.C. 1977), 12n

Blackham v. Gresham 16 F. 609 (C.C.N.Y. 1883), 12n

Bluefield Waterworks & Improvement Co. v. Public Serv. Comm'n, 262 U.S. 679 (1923), 85n

Federal Power Commission v. Hope Natural Gas Co., 320 U.S. 591 (1944), 85

Fort Wayne Community Schools v. Fort Wayne Ed. Ass'n, Inc., 977 F.2d 358 (7th Cir. 1992), 22n

Humphrey's Executor v. United States, 295 U.S. 602 (1935), 96, 96n

Hush-A-Phone Corp. v. United States, 238 F.2d 266 (D.C. Cir. 1956), 33, 33n

Ex parte Jackson, 96 U.S. (6 Otto)

727 (1878), 12n

Mackie v. Bush, 809 F. Supp. 144 (D.D.C. 1993), 96n
Mackie v. Clinton, 827 F. Supp. 56 (D.D.C. 1993), 96n
Mail Classification Schedule, 1995, Classification Reform I, Dkt. No. MC 95-1 (Postal Rate Commission 1995), 106n
Mail Order Ass'n v. United States Postal Serv., 986 F.2d 509 (D.C. Cir. 1993), 97n

National Ass'n of Greeting Card Publishers v. United States Postal Serv., 569 F.2d 570 (D.C. Cir. 1976), 121, 121n, 122n
National Ass'n of Greeting Card Publishers v. United States Postal Serv., 607 F.2d 392 (D.C. Cir. 1978), 123n
National Ass'n of Greeting Card Publishers v. United States Postal Serv., 462 U.S. 810 (1983), 123n
National Collegiate Athletic Ass'n v. Board of Regents of Univ. of Okla., 468 U.S. 85 (1984), 85n

Opinion and Recommended Decision, Dkt. No. R80-1 (Postal Rate Commission 1981), 110n

Perry Education Ass'n v. Perry Local Educators' Ass'n, 460 U.S. 37 (1983), 15n, 22n
Petrulis v. Commissioner, 938 F.2d 78 (7th Cir. 1991), 3n
Postal Rate and Fee Changes, 1990 Opinion and Recommended Decision, Dkt. No. R90-1 (Postal Rate Commission 1991), 91n
Postal Rate and Fee Changes, 1994, Dkt. No. R94-1 (Postal Rate Commission 1994), 21n, 48n, 92n, 118n
Powers v. United States Postal Serv., 671 F.2d 1041 (7th Cir. 1982), 2n
Pugsley v. Commissioner, 749 F.2d 691 (11th Cir. 1985), 3n

Regents of Univ. of Cal. v. Public Employment Relations Bd., 485 U.S. 589 (1988), 15n, 16n, 22n, 23
Reiter v. Sonotone Corp., 442 U.S. 330 (1979), 85n

In re Smith, 179 Bankr. 66 (W.D. Ohio
1995), 3n

United States v. Black, 569 F.2d 1111 (10th Cir. 1978) 1910), 12n
United States v. E. I. du Pont de Nemours & Co., 351 U.S. 377 (1956), 98n
United States v. Erie R.R., 235 U.S. 513 (1915), 22n, 23n
United States v. Pittsburg, 661 F.2d 783 (9th Cir. 1981), 3n
United States v. Thompson, F. Cas. No. 16489 (D. Mass. 1846), 12n
United States Postal Serv. v. Brennan, 574 F.2d 712 (2d Cir. 1978), 12n
United States Postal Serv. v. Council of Greenburgh Ass'ns,

453 U.S. 114 (1981), 15n, 35,
  35n, 36, 36n, 37n, 38
United States Postal Serv. *v.*
  O'Brien, 644 F. Supp. 140
  (D.D.C. 1986), 27n

Williams *v.* Wells Fargo & Co.
  Express, 177 F. 352 (8th Cir.
  1910), 12n

Name Index

Adie, Douglas K., 76n, 94n
Alberta, Paul M., 78n

Baumol, William J., 16n, 41n, 46n,
    55n, 57n, 63n, 107n, 108n,
    125n, 126n, 130, 130n, 138n
BeVier, Lillian R., 35n
Berg, Sanford B., 40n
Bork, Robert H., 85n
Bowles, Scott, 79n
Bowsher, Charles A., 6n
Bradford, David F., 125n, 126n
Braeutigam, Ronald R., 102n
Bush, George, 96

Carlton, Dennis W., 40n, 42n
Castaneda, Ruben, 79n
Chandler, Alfred D., 67, 67n
Chronis, Peter G., 2n
Coase, Ronald H., 11
Costich, Rand, 88n
Coverdell, Paul, 32
Crandall, Robert W., 51n, 73n

Crew, Michael A., 46n, 61n,
    104n, 107n
Cullinan, Gerald, 65n

Davis, O. A., 126n
Devins, Neal, 96n
Douglas, William O., 85

Ely, Bert, 152n

Feldstein, Martin S., 126n
Fisher, Christy, 150n
Franzen, Jonathan, 77n, 81n
Fuller, Wayne E., 44n, 62n
Fuss, Melvyn A., 118n

Geddes, R. Richard, 84n, 88n, 89n,
    96n
George, Anthony, 126n
Ginsburg, Douglas H., 52n
Gleiman, Edward J., 84n

Haldi, John, 12, 13n
Hall, George R., 105n, 107n
Hansmann, Henry B., 67n
Hiltzik, Michael A., 31n
Houston, Paul, 32n
Huber, Peter W., 33n
Hyman, Leonard S., 8n

Jensen, Michael C., 140n

Kahn, Alfred E., 16n
Karpoff, Jonathan M., 79n
Kellogg, Michael A., 33n
Klein, Benjamin, 76n
Kleindorfer, Paul R., 46n, 61n, 104n, 107n

Landes, William E., 128n
Leffler, Keith B., 76n
Lerner, Abba P., 126n
Lewis, Tracy R., 102n
Lloyd, Janine, 72n
Locy, Toni, 79n
Lott, John R., 80n

McAllister, Bill, 7n, 31n, 33n, 78n, 149n
MacAvoy, Paul W., 2n, 16n, 68, 68n, 73n
McHugh, John, 6n 79n, 99n
McIsaac, George S., 2n, 68, 68n
Makovic, Eugene, 32n
Maloney, Michael T., 80n
Mayton, William Ty, ix, 11n, 62n, 83n, 89n, 121n
Milgrom, Paul, 63n, 140n
Mill, John Stuart, 48, 49n
Miller, Bill, 78n
Mitchell, Bridger M., 101n
Mitchell, Mark L., 80n

Nomani, Asra Q., 7n, 149n

Oster, Sharon M., 46n, 89n
Owen, Bruce M., 46n

Panzar, John C., 41n, 45n, 46n, 55n, 102n, 108n
Perloff, Jeffrey M., 40n, 42n, 76n
Phelps, Edith M., 6n
Posner, Richard A., 128n
Praeger, Frederick A., 65n
Priest, George L., 11n, 61n, 94n, 95n

Ramsey, Frank P., 125n
Rehnquist, William, 15, 17, 17n, 36
Roberts, John, 63n, 140n
Rogers, James A., 6n
Rogerson, Cathy M., 45n
Runyon, Marvin, 5, 5n, 7n, 32, 59, 59n, 78n, 89, 97n, 119, 119n, 124, 139n, 150, 150n
Rush, Tonda F., 149n

Sappington, David E. M., 102n
Schwartz, Marius, 7n
Scott, Frank A., Jr., 126n, 132n
Scott, George C., 74n
Sherman, Roger, 40n, 94n, 118n, 125n, 126n
Shogan, Robert, 32n
Sidak, J. Gregory, 16n, 46n, 50n, 52n, 55n, 57n, 61n, 83n, 104n, 107n, 108n, 130n, 138n
Smith, Kerri S., 2n
Smith, Marshall, 72n
Spence, A. Michael, 136, 137n
Spulber, Daniel F., 16n, 40n, 42n, 55n, 63n, 67n, 107n, 110n, 126n, 142n

Stangle, Bruce E., 16n
Stigler, George J., 45n, 63n, 156n
Stiglitz, Joseph E., 7n

Takis, William M., 45n
Thorne, John, 33n
Tierney, John T., 89n, 90, 90n, 94n, 117n
Tirole, Jean, 41n
Tolley, George S., 129, 129n
Train, Kenneth E., 40n
Tschirhart, John, 41n
Tye, William B., 132n

Upton, Fred, 32n

Vickers, John, 61n
Vogelsang, Ingo, 101n

Wachter, Michael L., 76n
Waverman, Leonard, 126n, 131, 131n
Wheeler, Linda, 78n, 79n
Whinston, A. B., 126n
Willette, Gail, 88n
Williamson, Oliver E., 63n
Willig, Robert D., 41n, 46n, 55n, 63n, 108n
Wolf, Eric D., 7n

Yarrow, George, 61n

Subject Index

Acquiescence, 10, 147–51, 162
Advertising circulars, 19, 149
  unaddressed, 7, 58, 149
Advo, Inc., 149
Air Express International, 65, 148
Airborne Express, 4, 65, 148
Alternate Postal Delivery, Inc., 66, 148
American Airlines, 3, 23
American Freightways, 65
Antitrust laws, 1, 84, 85, 153, 157, 158, 161–62
AT&T, 33, 156
Automation, 67–69

Bar codes, 21, 68
  in tracking systems, 75
Bar coding, 19, 68, 69
Barriers to entry, 64, 65, 120, 127, 135, 153
  economic, 63
  legal, 3, 135, 136
  regulatory, 3, 43, 92, 118, 126, 133, 135

  statutory, 3, 120, 129, 135, 151, 153
  technological, 62, 63
    absence of, 38, 46, 63–66, 81
BellSouth Corporation, 158
Bell System, 31, 36, 72, 156

Cable & Wireless plc, 158
Capital recovery, 16, 64
Cargo, 21
Carriers
  alternative advertising, 57, 58
  city delivery, 110
  letter, 111
  of last resort, 73, 155
  private, 3, 4, 5, 15, 32, 40, 47, 57, 86, 135
  regulatory exclusion of, 40
  rural, 110
Citicorp, 3
Collection, 14, 47
  dispersed, 63
  local, 43, 45, 47, 52–54, 55, 60

Commercialization, 10, 140, 147, 152–59, 162, 163
   abroad, 157–59
Compensation, 24
Competition, 8, 9, 12, 19, 19, 51, 58, 59, 70, 88, 89, 105, 119, 120, 123, 130, 131, 132, 134, 136, 137, 138, 140, 148, 150, 152, 153, 154, 156, 157, 162
   protecting from the postal monopoly, 1, 10, 163
   restricting, 13, 18
   suppressing, 21, 55
Competitive markets, 41, 70, 75, 87, 92, 102, 103, 119, 120, 140
   entry into, 1, 5, 6, 14, 57, 65, 66, 71, 120, 138, 147, 150
   suppression of, 16
   exit from, 56, 161
   regulation of, 87
Comsat, 7
Consolidated Freightways, 65, 148
Consumer price index (CPI), 103
Consumer welfare, 38, 85, 136, 137, 140, 154, 157
Constructed marginal cost measure, 115
Content, 23, 36, 56
Con-Way, 148
Corporate governance, 1
Cost
   allocation, 4, 58, 86, 111, 119, 126, 127, 128, 140, 144
   attributable, 10, 86, 107, 109–15, 116, 119, 124, 126, 131, 139, 141, 144, 145, 151
   average, 42, 50, 142, 143
   delivery, 52, 72, 109
   duplication of, 40
   of entry, 57, 58, 63, 134
   fixed, 20, 42, 43, 51, 91, 104, 109, 110, 111, 114, 118, 124, 141, 142, 145
   incremental, 108, 119, 124
   institutional, 92, 107, 109–15, 119, 126, 127, 130, 131, 136, 138, 139, 151
   of the Postal Service, 115–19
   joint and common, 56, 109, 110, 111, 116, 118, 124, 126, 131, 132, 141, 142, 144, 145, 146
   labor, 68, 69, 95, 116
   marginal, 42, 114, 115, 124, 125, 128, 141, 142, 144, 145, 151
   minimization of, 43, 66, 67, 70, 89, 94, 103, 105
   misallocation of, 10, 93, 105–24, 126, 138, 140, 141, 145, 151
      anticompetitive, 101–05
      and Ramsey pricing, 140–46
      remedies for, 123–24
   nonattributable, 116–17
   operating, or "variable," 43, 70, 106, 109, 114, 115
   opportunity, 20, 21, 130
   recovery of, 10, 20, 63, 67, 86, 91, 107, 124, 141, 142, 146
   stand-alone, 55, 56, 57, 58, 103, 107, 108, 120, 145
   subadditive, 41
   sunk, 63, 64
   total, 18, 43, 105, 106, 107, 110, 114, 116, 118, 124, 125, 138, 141, 142, 143, 144, 145
   transactional, 63, 72
   volume-sensitive, 109
Cost calculation,
   constructed marginal cost measure, 115
   volume-variable method, 114–15
Cost drivers, 111, 115
Cost functions, 40, 141
   attributable, 141
   long-run, 42
   natural monopoly, 39, 42

Subject Index 189

variable, 114
Cost tests
   incremental, 108-09
   stand-alone, 107-08
Criminal punishment, 13-15, 18, 30
   of postal employees, 77, 80
Cross-subsidization, 74, 89, 104, 108, 109, 110, 111, 115, 119, 120, 145, 155, 162
   anticompetitive, 101-04, 151, 152
   preventing, 119-20

Delivery, 25, 34, 39, 40, 43, 62, 63, 65, 72, 75, 109
   of advertising circulars, 149
   air, 148
   alternative, 35
   of bills, 34
   dispersed, 63
   door-to-door, 47, 48-52
   of first class mail, 11, 120, 134, 135, 138
   frequency of, 50, 51
   high-cost, 72, 73, 155, 162
   of letter mail, 1, 19, 20, 29, 50, 57, 58, 81, 92, 100, 148, 151
   local, 43, 45, 55, 57, 60, 149
   of mail, 26, 34, 37, 38, 42, 43, 51, 53, 58, 69, 72, 77, 111, 115, 117, 152, 154, 156
   postal, 62, 63, 65, 81, 92, 109, 155
   Postal Service monopoly over, 3
   private express, 35
   by private messenger, 34
   regional, 46
   second-day, 148
   sorting, 68
   time, 29
   timeliness of, 26, 27, 29
   test of, 28
Delta Airlines, 3
DHL, 4, 65, 148

Dividends, 2, 67, 88, 139
Due process
   in postal regulation, 85
   in utility regulation, 85
Duplication
   of effort, 48
   of facilities, 43, 56
Du Pont, 3

Economic welfare, 10, 66, 124, 125, 147, 151, 152, 155, 162
Economies
   cost, 66, 70
   network, 47
   organizational, 44
   of scale, 42, 45, 46, 48, 49, 50, 51, 52, 54, 60, 67, 70, 114, 118, 124, 142, 143
   local, 46
   of scope, 39, 40, 55-58, 60, 67, 118, 138
   vertical, 46
Efficiency, 25, 43, 44, 66, 67, 72, 81, 83, 102, 104, 130
   cost, 9, 39, 41, 54, 91
   losses in, 48
   static, 41
   technical, 67
   transactional, 22
Elasticity
   of cost, 11, 114
   of demand, 126-130, 132, 133-37, 138, 143, 144, 151
   defined, 128
   inverse, 121-23, 124
   price, 106
   of supply, 134
Electronic commerce, 7, 53, 75, 131, 150
Emery/Purolator, 66, 148
Employee negligence, 76-80
Entrepreneurs, 15
Entry
   into competitive markets, 1, 5, 6, 16, 57, 65, 66, 71, 119,

120, 134, 138, 147, 150
   suppression of, 16, 40
   private, 65
   into regulated markets, 17, 60
   regulation of, 9, 41, 43, 153
   restricting, 16, 21, 46, 55, 62, 70, 141
   scope of, 58
   technological barriers to, 40, 62, 63
Equifax, 31
Express carriers, 53, 147
   Postal Service leverage over, 30
   private, 25, 26, 29, 30, 31, 37, 57, 147
Externality, 160
   network, 46

Federal Communications Commission, 156, 159
Federal Express, 3, 4, 26, 28, 29, 31, 32, 34, 57, 59, 64, 65, 72, 75, 87, 148, 156, 161
Federal Trade Commission, 88, 157, 161
First Amendment, 35
Franking privileges, 109
Freedom of press, 35
Freedom of speech, 35

General Accounting Office (GAO), 4, 6, 8, 9, 10, 32, 58, 67, 68, 73, 95, 118, 124, 132, 134, 136, 137, 138, 150, 151
   GAO report on pricing, 4, 5, 6, 12, 72, 87, 118, 123, 126–33, 135, 137, 138
General Services Administration, 32
Grand Canyon, 71
Greyhound Lines, Inc., 65

Harte-Hanks Communications, Inc., 149

Havasupai Indian reservation, 71–72

Incentives
   for cost minimization, 66, 67, 70, 92, 105
   to cross-subsidize, 101, 103, 104, 120, 151
   economic, 109
   for entry, 92
   for growth, 94, 103
   for innovation, 92, 103
   oversight, 67, 92
   performance, 91, 102–03
   for productive efficiency, 66, 82
   of U.S. Postal Service board of governors, 90
Incumbent burdens, 10, 16, 153, 154–56, 163
Inefficiency, 93, 118, 124, 139
   allocative, 37, 109
   cost, 9, 119
   economic, 123, 138
Information superhighway, 7, 150
Innovation, 9, 41, 49, 75, 92, 102, 103, 133
   losses in, 37
Insurance, 76
Integration,
   horizontal, 46
   vertical, 34
INTELSAT, 7
Internal Revenue Service (IRS), 2
Inverse elasticity rule, 4, 121, 122, 123, 124, 126–33, 136, 138, 143, 151
Investment, 42, 47, 54, 64, 65, 66, 67, 69, 86, 93, 139

Labor, 14, 48, 94, 109
   managerial, 14
Lee DataMail Services, 149
Legislation, 4, 159
   history of, 17, 18, 17, 83–84, 105

Subject Index 191

Letter
  accompanying cargo, 21–22
  carriage of before or after mailing, 21, 25
  carried out of mail, 13, 14, 20, 21
  of the carrier, 21, 22–23
  definition of, 12, 13, 18, 19
  extremely urgent, 26–31, 32
  and labelling, 28–29
  by private hands without compensation, 21, 23
  by special messenger, 24–25
  tracking of, 29

Mail
  bar-coded, 69, 96
  bulk, 7, 25, 26, 105, 149
  destruction and misappropriation of, 76–81
  electronic, 6, 9, 75, 150
  express, 1, 5, 13, 26, 28, 31, 32, 34, 55, 56, 57, 59, 72, 75, 87, 88, 89, 93, 94, 105, 106, 110, 116, 118, 119, 120, 134, 138, 141, 147, 148, 161
  extremely urgent, 26–31, 32, 156
  and labelling, 28–29
  failure to deliver, 80
  first class, 12, 26, 27, 39, 56, 57, 58, 77, 78, 93, 94, 96, 118, 120, 121, 122, 126, 129, 130, 131, 132, 133, 134, 135, 136, 138, 139, 141, 151
  fourth class, 56
  integrity of, 63, 74–81, 82
  letter, 1, 21, 37, 41, 46, 51, 55, 57, 66, 67, 70, 71, 73, 75, 81, 82, 84, 92, 100, 101, 105, 140, 150, 151, 152, 154, 155, 162, 163

  neighborhood, 149
  non-time-sensitive, 51
  presorted, 21
  priority, 148
  quality service of, 51
  reliability and security of, 62, 74–80, 81
  second class, 47, 52, 66, 122
  stolen, 79, 81
  third class, 12, 18–19, 56, 57, 66, 94, 138
  time-sensitive, 25
  undelivered, 77, 78, 79
  value of, 86
Mailbox, 33–36, 47, 52, 53, 153
  access, 34, 36, 37, 153
  aggregated, 52
  as a public forum, 35
Mail Boxes Etc., 48, 53
Mailmen, Inc., 149
Market failure, 59, 58, 60, 62, 87, 161
  scope of, 58
Market value, 9, 80, 87
Mid-America Mailers, Inc., 149
Monopoly
  over letter mail, 1, 3, 37, 39, 41, 50, 51, 55, 67, 71, 73, 84, 100, 101, 120, 140, 150, 155, 162, 163
  over mailbox access, 34, 153
  natural, 39, 40, 41, 47, 66, 70, 81, 118, 137, 160
    defined, 40–43
    unsustainable, 41
  postal, 1, 8, 10, 11, 12, 13, 15, 16, 17, 18, 19, 37, 57, 94, 137, 163
  and Private Express Statutes, 2, 5, 43–55, 60, 98, 100
  scope of, 12, 18, 19
  statutory, 10, 21, 37, 39, 40, 41, 51, 55, 60, 73, 74, 81, 84, 94, 101, 118, 119, 120, 124, 129, 130, 135,

138, 140, 141, 150, 153, 162

National Competitiveness Act, 32
National Newspaper Association, 149
Natural monopoly, 39, 40, 41, 47, 66, 70, 81, 118, 160
  defined, 40–43
  multiproduct, 55
  Postal Service as, 43–55, 60, 66, 80, 118, 137
  unsustainable, 41
Network, 41, 47, 56, 63
  electric power, 47, 63, 64
  and fixed costs, 43
  full-service, 46, 51–56
  hub-and-spoke system of, 25, 47, 56
  multiple vertical, 46
  physical, 42
  point-to-point system of, 56
  postal, 47
  and the Postal Service, 42, 63
  private express, 14, 15
  telecommunications, 47, 64
  transmission, 54, 63, 64
Nippon Telegraph & Telephone (NTT), 158

Occupational Safety and Health Administration (OSHA), 2
Optus Communications, Ltd., 158
Overnight mail,
  See also Mail, express
Oversight
  antitrust, 10, 153, 156–57, 159, 162, 163
  congressional, 95–96
  executive branch, 96–97
  of managerial performance, 67
  regulatory, 84, 101
  stricter, 10, 147, 159–62, 163

Parcel post, 1, 5, 6, 9, 51, 55, 56, 57, 59, 65, 72, 73, 75, 81, 87, 88, 89, 93, 94, 105, 106, 118, 119, 120, 134, 138, 141, 147
Pittston, 148
Postage, 6, 20, 29, 38, 97
Postal Inspection Service, 74
Postal monopoly,
  eliminating, 57
  expansion into new services, 1, 4, 6, 7, 38, 39, 55, 60, 71, 93, 118, 120, 138, 139, 147
  extension of, 6, 39, 40, 55, 57, 60
  preventing, 1
  natural monopoly justification for, 39, 40, 41, 48, 137
  technological justifications for, 10, 39–60
Postal Rate Commission, 5, 6, 50, 84–88, 90, 91, 95, 96, 97, 98, 104, 105, 106, 107, 109, 110, 117, 120, 122, 123, 129, 131, 155, 156, 159, 160, 161, 162, 163
  strengthening, 159–60
Postal reorganization, 67, 69, 84, 89, 92, 94, 95, 101, 117, 127
Postal Reorganization Act of 1970, 70, 72, 83, 85, 89, 94, 95, 100, 105, 120, 121, 127
Presorting, 19, 25, 26, 68, 69
  discounting, 48
Price
  absolute or relative, 26, 27–28
  caps
    logic of, 102–04
    and the Postal Service, 104–05
    regulation, 101–05
  ceiling, 103
  floors, 13, 28
  uniform, 16, 18, 154, 162
Price Waterhouse, 78

Subject Index   193

Pricing
  demand-based, 127, 128, 130, 132
  flexibility, 4, 5, 6, 102, 119, 124, 138, 139
  inverse elasticity, 12, 87, 120-23, 137, 140, 141
  marginal cost, 124, 143
  uniform, 63, 70-74, 81, 109
  value-of-service, 87
  See also Ramsey pricing
Private Express Statutes, 1, 2, 5, 10, 12, 13, 14, 15, 16, 17, 18-19, 34, 37, 38, 41, 57, 60, 70, 84, 98, 134, 135, 136, 137, 140, 141, 152, 159
  and competition, 1, 19
  enforcement of, 31-33, 71, 154
  exceptions to and exemptions from, 13, 19-31
  and monopoly, 2, 5, 43-55, 60, 98, 100
  repeal of, 153-54, 155, 162
  suspension of, 26, 30, 31
  and third class mail, 18-19
Privatization, 61
  postal, 5, 10, 141, 147, 151-52, 159, 163
Profit, 6, 85, 92, 93, 100, 102, 105
  margin, 91, 103
  maximization, 13, 67, 81, 88, 89, 94, 105, 118, 120, 152, 160
  monopoly, 137, 138, 152
  Postal Service's pursuit of, 5, 67, 92, 137-140, 159
Public control of the Postal Service, 41, 46, 58, 67, 72, 75, 83, 91
  congressional oversight, 83, 95-96
  executive branch oversight, 83, 96-97
  managerial control, 67, 83, 88-95
  natural monopoly

  justification for, 39
  regulatory control, 83, 84-88, 89, 90
Public enterprise, 7, 11, 12, 59, 87, 105, 124, 141, 152, 153, 157, 160, 161
  commercialized, 158
  U.S. Postal Service as, 18, 79, 88, 90, 94, 151, 156, 159
Public utilities, 8, 9, 34, 74
  abroad, 8
  regulation of, 8, 83, 84-88, 90, 101
Publishers Express, Inc., 66

Ramsey pricing, 115, 123, 124-26, 130, 137, 138, 140, 151
  and cost misallocation, 140-46
  misuse of, 10, 124-37
Rate structure, 107, 109, 119, 155
  of the Postal Service, 109, 123, 131
  regulatory, 86, 107, 108
  subsidy-free, 107, 108, 110, 145
Regulation
  cost-of-service, 101, 106-07
  of entry, 9, 40, 41, 153
  history of, 38
  of mailboxes, 33-38
  postal, 12, 13, 15, 43, 85-88, 141
  of postal rates, 4, 84-88, 140
  price-cap, 101-05
  of quality of postal services, 50
  rate-of-return, 104, 106
  utility, 8, 83, 84-88, 90, 101
Regulatory lag, 102, 103, 105
  and inflation, 103
Reliability, 62, 74-80, 81
Reputational harm, 75-80
Returns to scale
  competitive, 86
  constant, 45
  decreasing, 45, 49

increasing, 40, 70
Revenue requirement, 91, 106, 107
  break-even, 6, 91, 92, 105, 106
  regulatory, 86
Roadway Services, Inc., 65, 148

Safeway, 45
Scale, 23
Scope, 23
  efficient, 59
  geographic, 59
  national, 54
  regional, 54
Search and seizure, 2, 31, 38, 156
Security
  of the mail stream, 62, 74–80, 81
Sortation, 40, 68, 69, 109
  centralized, 63
  equipment, 54, 64, 68, 116
  local, 43, 45–48, 55, 60
  regional 42, 43, 51
Special messenger, 24–25
Supreme Court, 11, 15–18, 22, 23, 35, 36, 123

Taxes, 97, 153, 154–55, 160
  income, 2, 157, 158
  stamp, 97
Technology
  known, 40, 42, 48
  least-cost production, 17
  of mail delivery, 41, 62, 66
  natural monopolistic properties, 39, 41, 43–55, 56, 118
  obsolete, 9
Telstra Corporation Ltd., 157, 158
Texaco, 3
Time Warner's Publishers Express, Inc., 66
Timeliness of delivery, 26, 27, 29
  test, 28
Timeliness-by-distance test, 29

Transportation, 9, 14, 40, 41–42, 43, 53, 63, 75, 109
  long-distance, 43–44, 45, 46, 55, 60
  regional, 43, 44–45, 46, 55, 60
  services, 62

Ubiquity, 63, 70–74, 81
Uniformity, 63, 70–74, 81
United Airlines, 3, 22, 23
United Parcel Service (UPS), 4, 26, 28, 29, 34, 57, 59, 64, 65, 72, 75, 87, 148, 161
Universal service, 16, 17, 36, 62, 70–74, 81, 82, 154–56
University of California, 23
U.S. Court of Appeals,
  for District of Columbia Circuit, 19, 96–97, 121–23
U.S. Criminal Code, 13, 33
U.S. Department of Justice, 96–97, 131
  Antitrust Division, 88, 157, 162
U.S. Postal Service
  Board of Governors, 53, 89–91, 95, 96, 97, 99
  expansion of, 1, 4, 6, 7, 38, 39, 55, 60, 71, 93, 118, 120, 138, 139, 147
  as natural monopoly, 43–55, 60, 66, 81, 137
  privatizing, 5, 10, 141, 147, 151–52, 159, 163
  as "profit center" for federal government, 5, 67, 92, 139, 159, 160, 163
  protection from competition, 1, 89
  as public enterprise, 18, 79, 88, 90, 94, 151, 156, 159
  reputation of, 79
U.S. Treasury, 2, 92
  borrowing from, 2, 95, 153

Wal-Mart, 45
Western Electric, 33

Zip codes, 68

Board of Trustees

Wilson H. Taylor, *Chairman*
Chairman and CEO
CIGNA Corporation

Tully M. Friedman, *Treasurer*
Hellman & Friedman

Edwin L. Artzt
Chairman of the Executive Committee
The Procter & Gamble
 Company

Joseph A. Cannon
Chairman and CEO
Geneva Steel Company

Raymond E. Cartledge
Retired Chairman and CEO
Union Camp Corporation

Albert J. Costello
President and CEO
W. R. Grace & Co.

Christopher C. DeMuth
President
American Enterprise Institute

Malcolm S. Forbes, Jr.
President and CEO
Forbes Inc.

Christopher B. Galvin
President and COO
Motorola, Inc.

Robert F. Greenhill
Chairman and CEO
Smith Barney Inc.

M. Douglas Ivester
President and COO
The Coca-Cola Company

James W. Kinnear
Former President and CEO
Texaco Incorporated

Martin M. Koffel
Chairman and CEO
URS Corporation

Bruce Kovner
Chairman
Caxton Corporation

Kenneth L. Lay
Chairman and CEO
ENRON Corp.

Marilyn Ware Lewis
Chairman
American Water Works Company, Inc.

The American Enterprise Institute for Public Policy Research

Founded in 1943, AEI is a nonpartisan, nonprofit, research and educational organization based in Washington, D.C. The Institute sponsors research, conducts seminars and conferences, and publishes books and periodicals.

AEI's research is carried out under three major programs: Economic Policy Studies; Foreign Policy and Defense Studies; and Social and Political Studies. The resident scholars and fellows listed in these pages are part of a network that also includes ninety adjunct scholars at leading universities throughout the United States and in several foreign countries.

The views expressed in AEI publications are those of the authors and do not necessarily reflect the views of the staff, advisory panels, officers, or trustees.

Alex J. Mandl
Executive Vice President
AT&T

Craig O. McCaw

Paul H. O'Neill
Chairman and CEO
Aluminum Company of America

Paul F. Oreffice
Former Chairman
Dow Chemical Co.

George R. Roberts
Kohlberg Kravis Roberts & Co.

John W. Rowe
President and CEO
New England Electric System

Edward B. Rust, Jr.
President and CEO
State Farm Insurance Companies

James P. Schadt
President & CEO
The Reader's Digest Association, Inc.

John W. Snow
Chairman, President, and CEO
CSX Corporation

Henry Wendt
Chairman
The Finisterre Fund

James Q. Wilson
James A. Collins Professor
 of Management
University of California
 at Los Angeles

Officers

Christopher C. DeMuth
President

David B. Gerson
Executive Vice President

Council of Academic Advisers

James Q. Wilson, *Chairman*
James A. Collins Professor
 of Management
University of California
 at Los Angeles

Gertrude Himmelfarb
Distinguished Professor of History
 Emeritus
City University of New York

Samuel P. Huntington
Eaton Professor of the
 Science of Government
Harvard University

D. Gale Johnson
Eliakim Hastings Moore
 Distinguished Service Professor
 of Economics Emeritus
University of Chicago

William M. Landes
Clifton R. Musser Professor of
 Economics
University of Chicago Law School

Sam Peltzman
Sears Roebuck Professor of Economics
  and Financial Services
University of Chicago
  Graduate School of Business

Nelson W. Polsby
Professor of Political Science
University of California at Berkeley

George L. Priest
John M. Olin Professor of Law and
  Economics
Yale Law School

Murray L. Weidenbaum
Mallinckrodt Distinguished
  University Professor
Washington University

Research Staff

Leon Aron
Resident Scholar

Claude E. Barfield
Resident Scholar; Director, Science
  and Technology Policy Studies

Cynthia A. Beltz
Research Fellow

Walter Berns
Resident Scholar

Douglas J. Besharov
Resident Scholar

Jagdish Bhagwati
Visiting Scholar

Robert H. Bork
John M. Olin Scholar in Legal Studies

Karlyn Bowman
Resident Fellow

John E. Calfee
Resident Scholar

Richard B. Cheney
Senior Fellow

Lynne V. Cheney
W. H. Brady, Jr., Distinguished Fellow

Dinesh D'Souza
John M. Olin Research Fellow

Nicholas N. Eberstadt
Visiting Scholar

Mark Falcoff
Resident Scholar

John D. Fonte
Visiting Scholar

Gerald R. Ford
Distinguished Fellow

Murray F. Foss
Visiting Scholar

Suzanne Garment
Resident Scholar

Jeffrey Gedmin
Research Fellow

Patrick Glynn
Resident Scholar

Robert A. Goldwin
Resident Scholar

Robert W. Hahn
Resident Scholar

Robert B. Helms
Resident Scholar; Director, Health
  Policy Studies

James D. Johnston
Resident Fellow

Jeane J. Kirkpatrick
Senior Fellow; Director, Foreign and
  Defense Policy Studies

Marvin H. Kosters
Resident Scholar; Director,
  Economic Policy Studies

Irving Kristol
John M. Olin Distinguished Fellow

Dana Lane
Director of Publications

Michael A. Ledeen
Resident Scholar

James Lilley
Resident Fellow; Director, Asian
  Studies Program

Chong-Pin Lin
Resident Scholar; Associate Director,
  Asian Studies Program

John H. Makin
Resident Scholar; Director, Fiscal
  Policy Studies

Allan H. Meltzer
Visiting Scholar

Joshua Muravchik
Resident Scholar

Charles Murray
Bradley Fellow

Michael Novak
George F. Jewett Scholar in Religion,
  Philosophy, and Public Policy;
  Director, Social and
  Political Studies

Norman J. Ornstein
Resident Scholar

Richard N. Perle
Resident Fellow

William Schneider
Resident Scholar

William Shew
Visiting Scholar

J. Gregory Sidak
F. K. Weyerhaeuser Scholar

Herbert Stein
Senior Fellow

Irwin M. Stelzer
Resident Scholar; Director, Regulatory
  Policy Studies

W. Allen Wallis
Resident Scholar

Ben J. Wattenberg
Senior Fellow

Carolyn L. Weaver
Resident Scholar; Director, Social
  Security and Pension Studies